DEFENSE, SECURITY AND STRATEGIES

INFORMATION SECURITY AND CYBERSECURITY AT THE FEDERAL AVIATION ADMINISTRATION

CHALLENGES AND CONTROL EFFORTS

DEFENSE, SECURITY AND STRATEGIES

Additional books in this series can be found on Nova's website under the Series tab.

Additional e-books in this series can be found on Nova's website under the e-book tab.

DEFENSE, SECURITY AND STRATEGIES

INFORMATION SECURITY AND CYBERSECURITY AT THE FEDERAL AVIATION ADMINISTRATION

CHALLENGES AND CONTROL EFFORTS

EDITOR NAME

EDITOR

nova publishers

New York

NOTICE TO THE READER

Library of Congress Cataloging-in-Publication Data

ISBN: 978-1-63483-312-7

Published by Nova Science Publishers, Inc. † New York

CONTENTS

PREFACE

While the Federal Aviation Administration (FAA) has taken steps to protect its air traffic control systems from cyber-based and other threats, significant security control weaknesses remain, threatening the agency's ability to ensure the safe and uninterrupted operation of the national airspace system (NAS). These include weaknesses in controls intended to prevent, limit, and detect unauthorized access to computer resources, such as controls for protecting system boundaries, identifying and authenticating users, authorizing users to access systems, encrypting sensitive data, and auditing and monitoring activity on FAA's systems. Additionally, shortcomings in boundary protection controls between less-secure systems and the operational NAS environment increase the risk from these weaknesses. The objective of this book is to evaluate the extent to which FAA has effectively implemented information security controls to protect its air traffic control systems. This book also identifies the cybersecurity challenges facing FAA as it shifts to the NextGen ATC system and how FAA has begun addressing those challenges; and assesses the extent to which FAA and its contractors, in the acquisition of NextGen programs, have followed federal guidelines for incorporating cybersecurity controls.

In: Information Security and Cybersecurity ... ISBN: 978-1-63483-312-7
Editor: Victor Morris

Chapter 1

INFORMATION SECURITY: FAA NEEDS TO ADDRESS WEAKNESSES IN AIR TRAFFIC CONTROL SYSTEMS*

United States Government Accountability Office

ABBREVIATIONS

AIT	Office of Information and Technology
ARTCC	Air Route Traffic Control Center
ATC	Air Traffic Control
ATO	Air Traffic Organization
CIO	Chief Information Officer
ERAM	En Route Automation Modernization
FAA	Federal Aviation Administration
FISMA	Federal Information Security Management Act
FTI	FAA Telecommunications Infrastructure
IP	Internet Protocol
ISSO	Information System Security Officer
NAS	National Airspace System
NCO	NAS Cyber Operations
NextGen	Next Generation Air Transportation System

* This is an edited, reformatted and augmented version of The United States Government Accountability Office publication, GAO-15-221, dated January 2015.

NIST	National Institute of Standards and Technology
POA&M	Plan of Actions and Milestones
SBSS	Surveillance and Broadcast Service System
TFM-I	Traffic Flow Management-Infrastructure

WHY GAO DID THIS STUDY

In support of its mission, FAA relies on the NAS—one of the nation's critical infrastructures—which is comprised of air traffic control systems, procedures, facilities, aircraft, and people who operate and maintain them. Given the critical role of the NAS and the increasing connectivity of FAA's systems, it is essential that the agency implement effective information security controls to protect its air traffic control systems from internal and external threats.

GAO was asked to review FAA's information security program. Specifically, the objective of this review was to evaluate the extent to which FAA had effectively implemented information security controls to protect its air traffic control systems. To do this, GAO reviewed FAA policies, procedures, and practices and compared them to the relevant federal law and guidance; assessed the implementation of security controls over FAA systems; and interviewed officials. This is a public version of a report containing sensitive security information. Information deemed sensitive has been redacted.

WHAT GAO RECOMMENDS

GAO is making 17 recommendations to FAA to fully implement its information security program and establish an integrated approach to managing information security risk. In a separate report with limited distribution, GAO is recommending that FAA take 168 specific actions to address weaknesses in security controls. In commenting on a draft of this report, FAA concurred with GAO's recommendations.

WHAT GAO FOUND

While the Federal Aviation Administration (FAA) has taken steps to protect its air traffic control systems from cyber-based and other threats, significant security control weaknesses remain, threatening the agency's ability to ensure the safe and uninterrupted operation of the national airspace system (NAS). These include weaknesses in controls intended to prevent, limit, and detect unauthorized access to computer resources, such as controls for protecting system boundaries, identifying and authenticating users, authorizing users to access systems, encrypting sensitive data, and auditing and monitoring activity on FAA's systems. Additionally, shortcomings in boundary protection controls between less-secure systems and the operational NAS environment increase the risk from these weaknesses.

FAA also did not fully implement its agency-wide information security program. As required by the Federal Information Security Management Act of 2002, federal agencies should implement a security program that provides a framework for implementing controls at the agency. However, FAA's implementation of its security program was incomplete. For example, it did not always sufficiently test security controls to determine that they were operating as intended; resolve identified security weaknesses in a timely fashion; or complete or adequately test plans for restoring system operations in the event of a disruption or disaster. Additionally, the group responsible for incident detection and response for NAS systems did not have sufficient access to security logs or network sensors on the operational network, limiting FAA's ability to detect and respond to security incidents affecting its mission-critical systems.

The weaknesses in FAA's security controls and implementation of its security program existed, in part, because FAA had not fully established an integrated, organization-wide approach to managing information security risk that is aligned with its mission. National Institute of Standards and Technology guidance calls for agencies to establish and implement a security governance structure, an executive-level risk management function, and a risk management strategy in order to manage risk to their systems and information. FAA has established a Cyber Security Steering Committee to provide an agency-wide risk management function. However, it has not fully established the governance structure and practices to ensure that its information security decisions are aligned with its mission. For example, it has not (1) clearly established roles and responsibilities for information security for the NAS or

(2) updated its information security strategic plan to reflect significant changes in the NAS environment, such as increased reliance on computer networks.

Until FAA effectively implements security controls, establishes stronger agency-wide information security risk management processes, fully implements its NAS information security program, and ensures that remedial actions are addressed in a timely manner, the weaknesses GAO identified are likely to continue, placing the safe and uninterrupted operation of the nation's air traffic control system at increased and unnecessary risk.

* * *

January 29, 2015

Congressional Requesters

The Federal Aviation Administration (FAA) performs critical functions that contribute to ensuring safe, orderly, and efficient air travel in the national airspace system (NAS). Effective air traffic control (ATC) relies on automated systems and networks to provide information to air traffic controllers and aircraft flight crews to work toward ensuring safe and expeditious movement of aircraft. As a piece of critical infrastructure[1] within the nation's transportation sector,[2] the NAS is vitally important in supporting air traffic control operations nationwide, and disruptions could have a significant adverse impact.

Cyber-based threats to federal information systems such as those that FAA relies on for its ATC systems are evolving and growing. These threats can be intentional or unintentional and can come from a variety of sources, including criminals, foreign nations, terrorists, and other adversarial groups. For example, advanced persistent threats—where an adversary that possesses sophisticated levels of expertise and significant resources can attack by using multiple means such as cyber, physical, or deception to achieve its objectives[3]—pose increasing risks. Further, the growing interconnectivity among different types of information systems presents increasing opportunities for such attacks. Because of the increasing number of reported information security incidents, coupled with the advancement of security attacks, information and systems at FAA and across the government remain at risk.

Given the critical role the NAS plays in the nation's transportation sector and the growing threats to federal information systems, you asked us to review FAA's information security program. The specific objective of our review was to evaluate the extent to which FAA has effectively implemented appropriate information security controls to protect the confidentiality, integrity, and availability of its existing ATC systems.

This is a public version of a limited distribution report containing sensitive security information that we provided to you. Some of the information in the prior report has been designated as sensitive security information and must be protected from public disclosure. Therefore, this report does not contain detailed descriptions of the control weaknesses and related recommendations identified during our review. Although the information provided in this report is less detailed, it presents the same overall message as the limited distribution report. Also, the overall methodology used for both reports is the same.

To assess FAA's implementation of security controls on its existing ATC systems, we compared FAA's documented policies, procedures, and practices with the relevant information security law and federal guidance, including National Institute of Standards and Technology (NIST) standards and guidelines. We also assessed the implementation of controls over NAS supporting systems and interconnections by examining risk assessment processes, security plans, security control assessments, contingency plans, and remedial action plans. Specifically, we observed controls over the FAA Telecommunications Infrastructure (FTI), Surveillance and Broadcast Service System (SBSS), Traffic Flow Management-Infrastructure (TFM-I); En Route Automation Modernization (ERAM); and En Route Communications Gateway. We performed our work at FAA headquarters in Washington, D.C., and other locations supporting key systems, specifically: the Air Traffic Control Systems Command Center in Warrenton, Virginia; the FAA's William J. Hughes Technical Center in Egg Harbor Township, New Jersey; and at contractor facilities in Herndon, Virginia; Egg Harbor Township, New Jersey; and Melbourne, Florida.

We conducted this performance audit from August 2013 to January 2015 in accordance with generally accepted government auditing standards. Those standards require that we plan and perform the audit to obtain sufficient, appropriate evidence to provide a reasonable basis for our findings and conclusions based on our audit objectives. We believe that the evidence obtained provides a reasonable basis for our findings and conclusions based on our audit objective. A full description of our objective, scope, and methodology can be found in appendix I.

BACKGROUND

The FAA, an agency of the Department of Transportation, is primarily responsible for the advancement, safety, and regulation of civil aviation, as well as overseeing the development of the air traffic control system. Its stated mission is to provide the safest, most efficient aerospace system in the world. This system, known as the National Airspace System (NAS), includes air traffic control systems, ATC procedures, operational facilities, aircraft, and the people who certify, operate, and maintain them. According to FAA, the system includes more than 19,000 airports, nearly 600 air traffic control facilities, and approximately 65,000 other facilities, including radar, communications nodes, ground-based navigation aids, computer displays, and radios, intended to provide safe and efficient flight services for the public. Over 46,000 FAA personnel and approximately 608,000 pilots operate about 228,000 aircraft within the NAS, including up to 2,850 flights at any given moment. The system operates on a continuous basis, 24 hours a day, every day of the year.

As aircraft move across the NAS, controllers at several types of air traffic control facilities manage their movements during each phase of flight. According to FAA, these facilities include the following:

- More than 500 air traffic control towers supervise flights within about 5 miles from the airport runway. They give pilots taxiing and take off instructions, air traffic clearance, and provide separation between landing and departing aircraft.
- One hundred sixty Terminal Radar Approach Control facilities provide air traffic control services for airspace that is located within approximately 40 miles of an airport and generally up to 10,000 feet above the airport. These facilities handle sequencing and separation of aircraft as they approach major metropolitan areas.
- Twenty-two Air Route Traffic Control Centers (ARTCC) control and monitor airplanes over the continental United States and between airports. Controlling traffic usually at or above 17,000 feet, the typical center has responsibility for more than 100,000 square miles of airspace generally extending over a number of states. Three of the centers also control air traffic over the oceans. Controllers at these facilities work with pilots to ensure the flight path is smooth and free of other traffic.

- The Air Traffic Control System Command Center manages the flow of air traffic within the United States. This facility regulates air traffic when weather, equipment, runway closures, or other conditions place stress on the national airspace system. In these instances, traffic management specialists at the command center take action to modify traffic demands in order to keep traffic within system capacity.

Figure 1 provides a visual summary of air traffic control across the different phases of flight.

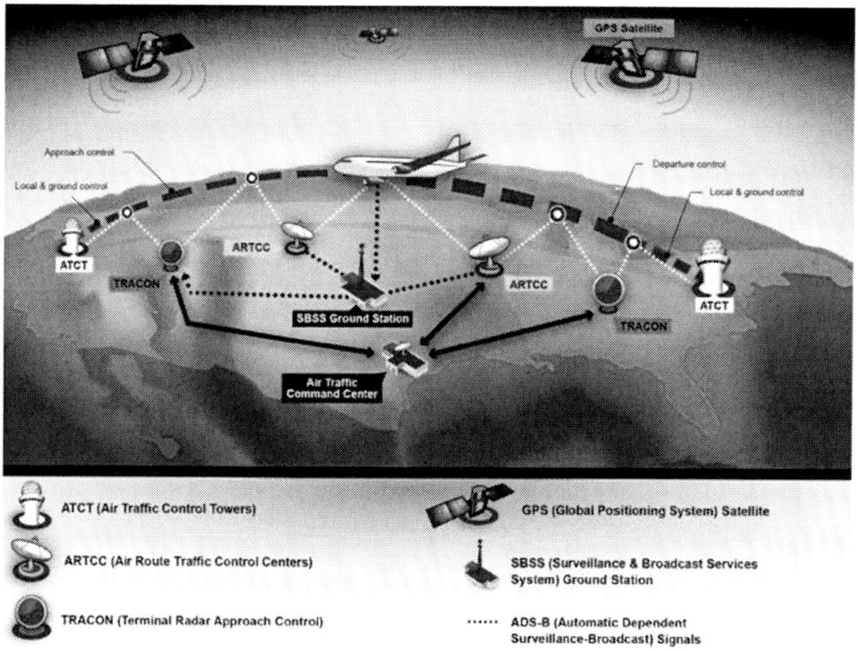

Source: GAO based on Federal Aviation Administration information. | GAO-15-221.

Figure 1. Summary of Air Traffic Control over the United States.

Many Networked Information Systems Support NAS Operations

The FAA's ability to fulfill its mission depends on the adequacy and reliability of its air traffic control systems, a vast network of computer hardware, software, and communications equipment. The agency relies on more than 100 air traffic control systems to process and track flights around the world. These complex and highly automated systems process a wide range of information, including radar, weather, flight plans, surveillance, navigation/landing guidance, traffic management, air-toground communication, voice, network management, and other information—such as airspace restrictions—that is required to support the agency's mission. In order to successfully carry out air traffic control operations, it is essential that these systems interoperate, functioning both within and across facilities as one integrated system of systems. According to FAA data available at the time of our review, about one-third of air traffic control systems rely on Internet Protocol (IP)-based networking technologies for communication.

FAA's ongoing effort to modernize the ATC system is referred to as the Next Generation Air Transportation System (NextGen). NextGen involves changes to many aspects of air transportation, including the acquisition of new integrated systems (both software and hardware), flight procedures, aircraft performance capabilities, and supporting infrastructure to transform the current air transportation system into one that uses satellite-based surveillance and navigation operations instead of ground-based radar. These changes are intended to increase the efficiency and capacity of the air transportation system while maintaining safety and accommodating anticipated future growth. As demand for the nation's increasingly congested airspace continues to grow, NextGen improvements are intended to enable the FAA to guide and track aircraft more precisely on more direct routes, reduce delays, save fuel, and reduce aircraft exhaust emissions.[4]

The following five key air traffic control systems perform critical air traffic control functions:

- FAA Telecommunications Infrastructure (FTI) forms the basic telecommunications infrastructure for NextGen, replacing the agency's legacy networks to provide consolidated telecom services for the NAS. The FTI is also intended to reduce costs, improve bandwidth, and offer improved information security services, such as encryption, so that an enterprise-wide approach to information security assurance can be achieved.
- Surveillance and Broadcast Service System (SBSS) provides surveillance services to FAA and the aviation community. Most notably, SBSS provides the Automatic Dependent Surveillance-Broadcast service—one of the six NextGen transformational programs—which is FAA's satellite-based successor to radar. This service makes use of Global Positioning System technology to

determine and share precise aircraft location information, and streams additional flight information to the cockpits of properly equipped aircraft.

- En Route Automation Modernization (ERAM) replaces the legacy en route Host computer and backup system, developed more than 40 years ago. According to FAA, much of the system has already been deployed. ERAM is designed to be at the heart of NextGen and is key to advancing FAA's transition from a ground-based system of air traffic control to a satellite-based system of air traffic management. As ERAM evolves, it is intended to provide benefits for users and the flying public by increasing air traffic flow and improving automated navigation and conflict detection services, both of which are vital to meeting future demand and preventing gridlock and delays.
- En Route Communications Gateway (ECG) is a communications system that receives data from sources outside the ARTCC, such as flight plan information and weather data, and passes it to other systems, including ERAM.
- Traffic Flow Management-Infrastructure (TFM-I) provides information processing support for FAA traffic management personnel as they coordinate the use of the NAS and respond to conditions of excess demand. TFM-I receives information on planned and active flights, generates forecasts of demand up to several hours ahead, presents this information to Traffic Management Personnel, and provides automation support for traffic management initiatives to resolve or ameliorate congestion.

Each of these systems, in conjunction with many others that make up the NAS computing infrastructure, works to ensure safe flight passageways for aircraft in U.S. airspace from takeoff to landing.

Information Security Is Critical to the Nation's Critical Infrastructures, Including Air Traffic Control Systems

Safeguarding federal computer systems and the systems supporting the nation's critical infrastructures, including the NAS, is essential to protecting national and economic security, and public health and safety. For government organizations information security is also a key element in maintaining the public trust. Inadequately protected systems may be vulnerable to insider threats as well as the risk of intrusion by individuals or groups with malicious intent who could use their illegitimate access to obtain sensitive information, disrupt operations, or launch attacks against other computer systems and networks. Accordingly, since 1997, we have designated information security as a government-wide high-risk area.[5] In 2003, we expanded this high-risk area to include protecting systems supporting our nation's critical infrastructure.[6] Our previous reports, and those of agency inspectors general, describe persistent information security weaknesses that place a variety of federal operations at risk of disruption, fraud, and inappropriate disclosure.

Recent federal guidance demonstrates that securing critical infrastructures from internal and external threats is a national priority. For example, in February 2013, the President signed Executive Order 13636, "Improving Critical Infrastructure Cybersecurity," to address concerns about better securing critical infrastructure from cyber threats. This order, among other things, directed executive branch agencies to promote the adoption of cybersecurity practices; increase the volume, timeliness and quality of cyber threat information sharing; incorporate privacy and civil liberties protections into every initiative to secure critical infrastructure; and explore the use of existing regulation to promote cybersecurity. The order also directed the National Institute of Standards and Technology (NIST) to develop a technology-neutral voluntary framework for improving critical infrastructure cybersecurity. The framework, issued in February 2014,[7] is designed to help organizations align their cybersecurity activities with business requirements, risk tolerances, and resources.

Although many legacy air traffic control systems continue to rely on point-to-point communications, NAS systems, including NextGen systems, increasingly use IP technologies to communicate over interconnected computer networks. With the increased use of such technologies, however, comes increased risk: integrating critical infrastructure systems with information technology networks provides significantly less isolation from the outside world than predecessor systems, creating a greater need to secure these systems from remote, external threats.

Several Organizations within FAA Are Responsible for Information Security

The operational arm of the FAA is the Air Traffic Organization (ATO), which is responsible for providing safe and efficient air navigation services to the nation's airspace. ATO is led by a Chief Operating Officer who reports directly to the FAA Administrator. The ATO includes seven service units: Air Traffic, Management, Mission Support, Program Management Organization, Safety and Technical Training, Systems Operations, and Technical Operations.

Several entities within ATO share responsibility for information security-related activities over air traffic control systems. The NAS Security Risk Executive is the individual with overall responsibility for overseeing all information security-related activities across ATO, including the security of air traffic control systems. ATO's Information Security Systems Group, within Technical Operations Services, includes NAS Cyber Operations (NCO), ISS Engineering, and an Authorization Team. Ensuring that each air traffic control system is properly secured and protected is the responsibility of an Information Systems Security Officer (ISSO), and the system owner is responsible for planning, directing, and managing resources for the system, including ensuring that the system meets all security requirements throughout its life cycle. The Security Risk Executive, Authorization Team, NCO, system owners, and ISSOs are jointly responsible for carrying out security program activities for NAS systems, including conducting system risk assessments, documenting system security plans, testing security controls, managing remedial action plans, monitoring and responding to incidents, and planning for contingencies.

The FAA Office of Information and Technology (AIT) is responsible for the security of FAA's non-NAS information systems. The office resides within FAA's Office of Finance and Management and is headed by the Chief Information Officer (CIO), who has overall responsibility to oversee the security of the agency's information and information systems. The FAA Chief Information Security Officer is responsible for developing, documenting, and implementing an agency-wide information security program and for assisting the CIO in ensuring compliance with federal law pertaining to information security and other applicable policies, standards, requirements and guidelines.

Requirements for Ensuring the Security of Federal Information Systems Are Established in Law and Guidance

Federal law and guidance specify requirements for protecting federal information and information systems. The Federal Information Security Management Act of 2002 (FISMA) requires each agency to develop, document, and implement an agency-wide information security program to provide security for the information and information systems that support operations and assets of the agency, including those provided or managed by another agency, contractor, or another organization on behalf of an agency.[8]

FISMA assigns certain responsibilities to NIST, which is tasked with developing, for systems other than national security systems, standards and guidelines that must include, at a minimum, (1) standards to be used by all agencies to categorize all of their information and information systems based on the objectives of providing appropriate levels of information security, according to a range of risk levels; (2) guidelines recommending the types of information and information systems to be included in each category; and (3) minimum information security requirements for information and information systems in each category.

Accordingly, NIST has developed a risk management framework of standards and guidelines for agencies to follow in developing information security programs. Relevant publications include the following:

- Federal Information Processing Standard 199, *Standards for Security Categorization of Federal Information and Information Systems*,[9] requires agencies to categorize their information systems as low-impact, moderate-impact, or high-impact for the security objectives of confidentiality, integrity, and availability. The potential impact values assigned to the respective security objectives are the highest values from among the security categories that the agency identifies for each type of information resident on those information systems.
- Federal Information Processing Standard 200, *Minimum Security Requirements for Federal Information and Information Systems*,[10] specifies minimum security requirements for federal agency information and information systems and a risk-based process for selecting the security controls necessary to satisfy these minimum security requirements.

- NIST Special Publication 800-34, *Contingency Planning Guide for Federal Information Systems*,[11] assists organizations in understanding the purpose, process, and format of information system contingency plan development through practical, real-world guidelines. While the principles establish a baseline to meet most organizational needs, it is recognized that each organization may have additional requirements specific to its own operating environment. This guidance document provides background information on interrelationships between information system contingency planning and other types of security and emergency management-related contingency plans, organizational resiliency, and the system development life cycle.
- NIST Special Publication 800-37, *Guide for Applying the Risk Management Framework to Federal Information Systems: A Security Life Cycle Approach*,[12] explains how to apply a risk management framework to federal information systems, including security categorization, security control selection and implementation, security control assessment, information system authorization, and security control monitoring.
- NIST Special Publication 800-39, *Managing Information Security Risk: Organization, Mission, and Information System View*,[13] provides guidance for an integrated, organization-wide program for managing information security risk to organizational operations (e.g., mission, functions, image, and reputation), organizational assets, individuals, other organizations, and the nation resulting from the operation and use of federal information systems. The guidance also provides a structured yet flexible approach for managing risk that is intentionally broad-based, with the specific details of assessing, responding to, and monitoring risk on an ongoing basis provided by other supporting NIST security standards and guidelines.
- NIST Special Publication 800-53, *Security and Privacy Controls for Federal Information Systems and Organizations*,[14] provides a catalog of security and privacy controls for federal information systems and organizations and a process for selecting controls to protect organizational operations, assets, individuals, other organizations, and the nation from a diverse set of threats including hostile cyber attacks, natural disasters, structural failures, and human errors. The guidance includes privacy controls to be used in conjunction with the specified

security controls to achieve comprehensive security and privacy protection.

- NIST Special Publication 800-82, *Guide to Industrial Control Systems (ICS) Security*,[15] provides guidance for securing industrial control systems, including supervisory control and data acquisition systems, distributed control systems, and other systems performing control functions. The document also provides an overview of industrial control systems and typical system topologies, identifies typical threats and vulnerabilities to these systems, and provides recommended security countermeasures to mitigate the associated risks. Because there are many different types of industrial control systems with varying levels of potential risk and impact, the document provides a list of many different methods and techniques for securing them.
- NIST Special Publication 800-100, *Information Security Handbook: A Guide for Managers*,[16] informs members of the information security management team (agency heads; CIOs; senior agency information security officers, also commonly referred to as chief information security officers; and security managers) about various aspects of information security that they will be expected to implement and oversee in their respective organizations. In addition, the handbook provides guidance for facilitating a more consistent approach to information security programs across the federal government.

SECURITY WEAKNESSES PLACE AIR TRAFFIC CONTROL SYSTEMS AT RISK

Although FAA has taken steps to safeguard its air traffic control systems, significant security control weaknesses remain in NAS systems and networks, threatening the agency's ability to adequately fulfill its mission. FAA established policies and procedures for controlling access to NAS systems and for configuring its systems securely, and it implemented firewalls and other boundary protection controls to protect the operational NAS environment. However, a significant number of weaknesses remain in the technical controls—including access controls, change controls, and patch management—that protect the confidentiality, integrity, and availability of its air traffic control systems. Additionally, significant interconnectivity exists between non-NAS systems and the NAS operational environment, increasing the risk from these weaknesses. Further, the agency had not yet fully implemented an agency-wide information security program to ensure that controls are appropriately designed and operating effectively. A key reason for both the technical control weaknesses and the security management weaknesses is that FAA had not fully established an integrated, organization-wide approach to managing information security risk that is aligned with its mission. These shortcomings put NAS systems at increased and unnecessary risk of unauthorized access, use, or modification that could disrupt air traffic control operations.

FAA Did Not Consistently Control Access to NAS Systems

A basic management objective for any agency is to protect the resources that support its critical operations and assets from unauthorized access. An agency can accomplish this by designing and implementing controls that are intended to prevent, limit, and detect unauthorized access to computer resources (e.g., data, programs, equipment, and facilities), thereby protecting them from unauthorized disclosure, modification, and loss. Specific access controls include boundary protection, identification and authentication of users, authorization restrictions, cryptography, and audit and monitoring procedures. Without adequate access controls, unauthorized users, including intruders and former employees, can surreptitiously read and copy sensitive data and make undetected changes or deletions for malicious purposes or for personal gain. In addition, authorized users could intentionally or unintentionally modify or delete data or execute changes that are outside of their authority.

Although FAA had issued security policies, it did not consistently protect its network boundary from possible intrusions; identify and authenticate users; authorize access to resources; ensure that sensitive data are encrypted; or audit and monitor actions taken on NAS systems and networks.

Although Control Mechanisms Were Put in Place, FAA Did Not Always Adequately Protect the Boundary of NAS Systems

Boundary protection controls are used to restrict connections into and out of networks and to control connections between network-connected devices. Implementing multiple layers of security to protect an information system's internal and external boundaries can reduce the risk of a successful cyber attack. For example, multiple firewalls can be deployed to prevent both outsiders and insiders from gaining unauthorized access to systems. NIST Special Publication 800-53[17] recommends organizations monitor and control communications both at the external boundary of the system and at key internal boundaries within the system. NIST also recommends information systems connect to external networks or systems only through managed interfaces such as gateways, routers, or firewalls. FAA policy states that connections between NAS systems/networks and any non-NAS network or non-NAS information systems must occur through the NAS Enterprise Security Gateway.

While FAA implemented numerous controls to separate NAS systems from non-NAS systems, it did not always sufficiently protect connections between external partners and NAS operational systems or limit interconnectivity between operational and mission support environments. The excessive interconnectivity between NAS and non-NAS environments increased the risk that FAA's mission-critical air traffic control systems could be compromised.

FAA Did Not Consistently Implement Controls for Identifying and Authenticating Users of NAS Systems

Information systems need to be managed to effectively control user accounts and identify and authenticate users. Users and devices should be appropriately identified and authenticated through the implementation of adequate logical access controls. Users can be authenticated using mechanisms such as a password and user ID combination. NIST SP 800- 53 recommends, and FAA policy requires, strong password controls for authentication, such as passwords that are at least eight alphanumeric characters in length, contain at least one upper- and one lower-case letter, contain numbers and special characters, and expire after a predetermined period of time.[18]

However, FAA did not consistently implement identification and authentication controls in accordance with its security policies and NIST guidance. For example, certain servers and applications supporting NAS systems did not implement sufficiently strong password controls. As a result, FAA is at increased risk that accounts could be compromised and used by unauthorized individuals to access sensitive information or systems.

FAA Did Not Always Ensure Users Were Properly Authorized to Access NAS Systems

Authorization encompasses access privileges granted to a user, program, or process. It is used to allow or prevent actions by that user based on predefined rules. Authorization includes the principles of legitimate use and least privilege.[19] NIST guidance recommends that organizations implement controls to ensure that only authorized users can access the system. This includes, but is not limited to, uniquely identifying all users, periodically reviewing access to the system, disabling accounts that no longer need access to the system, and assigning the lowest level of permission necessary for a task. NIST also recommends that systems and devices be configured so that only the functionality necessary to support organizational operations is enabled in order to prevent unauthorized connection of devices, unauthorized transfer of information, or unauthorized network connectivity.

FAA did not always ensure that users' access to key air traffic control systems was authorized in accordance with FAA policies and NIST guidance. In several cases, FAA and its contractors did not properly document that system users were authorized to access NAS systems. Additionally, FAA did not always ensure that periodic reviews of user access to NAS systems were performed in accordance with FAA policies and NIST guidance. As a result, users of these air traffic control systems may have greater access than they need to fulfill their responsibilities, increasing the risk that these systems could be compromised, either inadvertently or deliberately.

Sensitive Data Were Not Always Sufficiently Encrypted

Cryptographic controls can be used to help protect the integrity and confidentiality of data and computer programs by rendering data unintelligible to unauthorized users and/or protecting the integrity of transmitted or stored data. Cryptography involves the use of mathematical functions called algorithms and strings of seemingly random bits called keys to (1) encrypt a message or file so that it is unintelligible to those who do not have the secret key needed to decrypt it, thus keeping the contents of the message or file confidential; (2) provide an electronic signature that can be used to determine if any changes have been made to the related file, thus ensuring the file's integrity; and (3) link a message or document to a specific individual's or group's key, thus ensuring that the "signer" of the file can be identified. NIST guidance states that the use of encryption by organizations can reduce the probability of unauthorized disclosure of information. NIST Special Publication 800-53 recommends that organizations employ cryptographic mechanisms to prevent unauthorized disclosure of information during transmission, encrypt passwords while being stored and transmitted, and establish a trusted communications path between users and security functions of information systems. Additionally, when federal agencies employ cryptography, NIST standards require them to use Federal Information Processing Standard (FIPS) 140-2-validated algorithms.

FAA did not always ensure that sensitive data were encrypted when transmitted or stored, as called for by its policies and NIST guidance. For example, certain network devices supporting NAS systems did not always encrypt authentication data when transmitting them across the network, and other systems did not always encrypt stored passwords using sufficiently strong encryption algorithms in compliance with FIPS 140-2. Due to these weaknesses, FAA faces an increased risk that attackers could compromise accounts or intercept, view, and modify transmitted data, thereby threatening the confidentiality, integrity, and availability of the NAS.

FAA Did Not Consistently Implement Sufficient Audit and Monitoring Controls

Audit and monitoring involves the regular collection, review, and analysis of auditable events for indications of inappropriate or unusual activity, and the appropriate investigation and reporting of such activity. Automated mechanisms may be used to integrate audit monitoring, analysis, and reporting into an overall process for investigation of and response to suspicious activities. Audit and monitoring controls can help security professionals routinely assess computer security, perform investigations during and after an attack, and even recognize an ongoing attack. Audit and monitoring technologies include network- and host-based intrusion detection systems, audit logging, security event correlation tools, and computer forensics. Network-based intrusion detection systems capture or "sniff" and analyze network traffic in various parts of a network. FISMA requires that each federal agency implement an information security program that includes procedures for detecting, reporting, and responding to security incidents.

FAA did not consistently implement sufficient audit and monitoring controls. For example, FAA did not always have sufficient capability to monitor network traffic or ensure that NAS systems were sufficiently logging security-relevant events. As a result of these weaknesses, FAA faces an increased risk that it will be unable to detect and respond to unauthorized or malicious activities on its systems.

While Background Investigations Were Conducted in Accordance with Policy, Changes to Network Systems and Software Were Not Always Properly Controlled

In addition to access controls, other important controls should be in place to ensure the confidentiality, integrity, and availability of an agency's information. These controls include policies, procedures, and techniques for implementing personnel security and securely configuring information systems. While FAA conducted background investigations in accordance with its policy, weaknesses in its configuration management processes increase the risk of unauthorized use, disclosure, modification, or loss of sensitive information and information systems supporting FAA's mission.

FAA Conducted Background Investigations in Accordance with Policy

Policies related to personnel actions, such as hiring, termination, and maintaining employee expertise, are important considerations in securing information systems. If personnel policies are not adequate, an entity runs the risk of (1) hiring unqualified or untrustworthy individuals; (2) providing terminated employees opportunities to sabotage or otherwise impair entity operations or assets; (3) failing to detect continuing unauthorized employee actions; (4) lowering employee morale, which may in turn diminish employee compliance with controls; and (5) allowing staff expertise to decline. Hiring procedures should include contacting references, performing background investigations, and ensuring that periodic reinvestigations are consistent with the sensitivity of the position, in accordance with criteria from the Office of Personnel Management. FAA policy requires positions to be designated by sensitivity and risk level, and describes requirements for conducting background investigations for employees and contractors, including periodic reinvestigations of individuals in positions of higher risk or sensitivity.

FAA ensured that the employees and contractors we sampled on the TFM-I, ERAM, SBSS, and FTI programs had appropriate background investigations. Specifically, all of the employees and contractors we sampled had up-to-date background investigations that were consistent with the risk designation of their positions. As a result, FAA reduced its risk that it has employed or contracted for unqualified or untrustworthy individuals on these programs.

FAA Did Not Always Properly Control Changes to Network Devices or Ensure Key Systems Were Fully Patched

Configuration management is an important control that involves the identification and management of security features for all hardware and software components of an information system at a given point and systematically controls changes to that configuration during the system's life cycle. Configuration management involves, among other things, (1) verifying the correctness of the security settings in the operating systems, applications, or computing and network devices and (2) obtaining reasonable assurance that systems are configured and operating securely and as intended. In addition, establishing controls over the modification of information system components and related documentation helps to prevent unauthorized changes and ensure that only authorized systems and related program modifications are implemented. This is accomplished by instituting policies, procedures, and techniques that help make sure that all hardware, software, and firmware programs and program modifications have been properly authorized, tested, and approved. Patch management, a component of configuration management, is important for mitigating the risks associated with software vulnerabilities. When a software vulnerability is discovered, the software vendor may develop and distribute a patch or work-around to mitigate the vulnerability. Without the patch, an attacker can exploit the vulnerability to read, modify, or delete sensitive information; disrupt operations; or launch attacks against other systems. Outdated and unsupported software is more vulnerable to attack and exploitation because vendors may no longer provide updates, including security updates.

According to NIST SP 800-53, configuration management activities should include documenting approved configuration-controlled changes to information systems, retaining and reviewing records of the changes, auditing those records, and coordinating and providing oversight for configuration change control activities through a mechanism such as a change control board. Additionally, NIST Special Publication 800-128[20] states that patch management procedures should define how the organization's patch management process is integrated into configuration management processes, how patches are prioritized and approved through the configuration change control process, and how patches are tested for their impact on existing secure configurations. FAA policy describes detailed requirements for controlling changes to NAS systems.

FAA did not always ensure that changes to network devices supporting air traffic control systems were managed in accordance with FAA policies for configuration change control. Specifically, significant changes were made to a key network device on one NAS system without following the system's defined change control process, which requires that changes be documented, analyzed for potential security impacts, tested, and approved before being implemented. Without adequately controlling configuration changes to network devices, an increased risk exists that changes could be unnecessary, may not work as intended, or may result in unintentional side effects that could impact mission-critical operations.

Additionally, the agency did not always ensure that security patches were applied in a timely manner to servers and network devices supporting air traffic control systems, or that servers were using software that was up-to-date. For example, certain systems were missing patches dating back more than 3 years. Additionally, certain key servers had reached end-oflife and were no longer supported by the vendor. As a result, FAA is at an increased risk that unpatched vulnerabilities could allow its information and information systems to be compromised.

FAA Did Not Fully Implement Its Information Security Program, Limiting the Effectiveness of Information Security Controls

An entity-wide information security program is the foundation of a security control structure and a reflection of senior management's commitment to addressing security risks. The security program should establish a framework and continuous cycle of activity for assessing risk, developing and implementing effective security procedures, and monitoring the effectiveness of these procedures. Without a well-designed program, security controls may be inadequate; responsibilities may be unclear, misunderstood, or improperly implemented; and controls may be inconsistently applied. FISMA requires each agency to develop, document, and implement an information security program that, among other things, includes

- policies and procedures that (1) are based on risk assessments, (2) cost-effectively reduce information security risks to an acceptable level, (3) ensure that information security is addressed throughout the life cycle of each system, and (4) ensure compliance with applicable requirements;

- security awareness training to inform personnel of information security risks and of their responsibilities in complying with agency policies and procedures, as well as training personnel with significant security responsibilities for information security;
- periodic testing and evaluation of the effectiveness of information security policies, procedures, and practices, to be performed with a frequency depending on risk, but no less than annually, and that includes testing of management, operational, and technical controls for every system identified in the agency's required inventory of major information systems;
- a process for planning, implementing, evaluating, and documenting remedial actions to address any deficiencies in information security policies, procedures, or practices;
- procedures for detecting, reporting, and responding to security incidents; and
- plans and procedures to ensure continuity of operations for information systems that support the operations and assets of the agency.

To its credit, FAA has taken steps to implement an information security program and manage information security risks for its air traffic control systems. FAA produced system security plans for the systems we reviewed which specified the systems' operational contexts, relationships with others systems, general security requirements, and security controls. Additionally, FAA policy requires the periodic testing and evaluation of the controls on agency systems, and the agency has a process for planning, implementing, evaluating and documenting remedial actions to address deficiencies in those controls. FAA also documented a risk assessment policy and conducted risk assessments on the major systems we reviewed. However, FAA did not always consistently document incident response policies, ensure that contractors took required training, adequately test security controls, mitigate security weaknesses in a timely manner, ensure that incident response capabilities for NAS systems were adequate, or fully document and test contingency plans for its air traffic control systems.

Policies and Procedures Were Not Always Complete

A key element of an effective information security program is to develop, document, and implement risk-based policies, procedures, and technical standards that govern the security over an agency's computing environment. Regarding incident response activities, NIST Special Publication 800-53[21] recommends agencies create an incident response policy and procedures to facilitate the implementation of the policy and associated incident response controls.

Although FAA had developed and documented many information security policies and procedures, incident response policies and procedures were not always complete or approved. For example, although the NCO security group operates as the focal point for NAS incident response activities, ATO's incident response policy establishing NCO as the incident response focal point was still in draft at the time of our review. 22 Additionally, although system-level incident response policies had been finalized for four of the NAS systems we reviewed, they did not always specify incident reporting timeframes or the need for all incidents to be reported. Without finalized and harmonized incident response policies, FAA faces an increased risk that incident response authorities and responsibilities will not be clearly understood by all stakeholders, impeding the agency's ability to efficiently and effectively respond to incidents or to do so in a timely manner.

Users with Significant Security Responsibilities Had Not Always Received Required Security Training

According to FISMA, an agency-wide information security program must include security awareness training for agency personnel, contractors, and other users of information systems that support the agency's operations and assets. This training must cover (1) information security risks associated with users' activities and (2) users' responsibilities in complying with agency policies and procedures designed to reduce these risks. FISMA also includes requirements for training personnel who have significant responsibilities for information security. Additionally, NIST Special Publication 800-53 recommends that agencies provide incident response training to information system users consistent with their assigned roles and responsibilities.

Further, FAA policy states that all agency personnel and contractors must complete the agency's annual security awareness training, and that individuals with significant information system security responsibilities must receive role-based training specific to their responsibilities. For both security awareness and role-based training, FAA policy also states that records must be kept documenting the name and title of the individual receiving training, their security responsibilities, the type of training received, and the training date.

However, FAA did not always ensure that its employees and contractors took required information security training, including specialized security training and system-specific training, in a timely manner. For example:

- FAA contractors supporting certain NAS systems did not take the required security awareness training.
- Additionally, FAA did not provide periodic refresher security training to individuals with significant security responsibilities on two NAS systems. Although FAA stated that the Department of Transportation security awareness training, combined with on-the-job training, was sufficient, the Department of Transportation training does not cover security topics specific to these systems, and FAA did not define required content for on-the-job training or keep training records, as required by FAA policy.
- FAA had also not sufficiently documented that persons with incident response roles and responsibilities for one of the NAS systems we reviewed had taken required training, and did not provide formal incident response training for personnel on another NAS system.

Without adequately ensuring that personnel take required security training, FAA faces an increased risk that employees may not recognize and respond appropriately to potential security threats and vulnerabilities. Further, without sufficiently documenting that incident responders have taken required training, FAA faces an increased risk that employees will not receive training on performing their roles and responsibilities on a regular basis.

Security Controls Were Not Always Tested Sufficiently

FAA policy, in accordance with NIST guidance, states that security control assessments are to determine the extent to which controls are implemented correctly, operate as intended, and produce the desired outcome with respect to meeting the security requirements of the system. NIST Special Publication 800-53A[23] notes that while a high-level examination of a limited body of evidence can support an assessor's determination that a control is implemented and free of obvious errors, determining whether a control is implemented correctly and operating as intended requires an in-depth analysis of a substantial body of relevant evidence.

While FAA prepared assessments of the security controls for the NAS systems we reviewed, its control assessments were not always comprehensive enough to identify weaknesses that we found in user account management, configuration management, and security awareness training controls. For example, FAA concluded that the account review control for one system was implemented based on examining the system security plan and interviewing officials, but the testers did not examine artifacts such as audit reports to determine if reviews were being conducted as described in the security plan. FAA also concluded that configuration change control had been implemented for another system after examining the system security plan and interviewing personnel; however, artifacts such as change tickets and approval documents were not examined to determine if system changes were controlled in accordance with procedures. Further, FAA's test results indicated that the security awareness training common control was defined, but the testers did not examine training records to verify that personnel on the systems that rely on the control were taking the training as required. ATO officials stated that control assessments were often supported by additional documentation not described in the security control assessment reports; however, the agency was unable to provide evidence to corroborate this statement.

By not conducting more comprehensive tests of security controls, FAA has decreased assurance that controls are implemented correctly and operating as intended. Additionally, because security control assessments are used by agencies to evaluate whether contractors are implementing information security controls effectively, FAA had reduced assurance that its contractors were adequately securing and protecting air traffic control systems.

Identified Security Weaknesses Were Not Always Addressed in a Timely Fashion

FISMA requires that agency-wide information security programs include a process for planning, implementing, evaluating, and documenting remedial actions to address any deficiencies in the information security policies, procedures, and practices of the agency. Agencies must establish procedures to reasonably ensure that all information security control weaknesses, regardless of how or by whom they are identified, are addressed through the agency's remediation processes. For each identified control weakness, the agency is required to develop and implement a plan of actions and milestones (POA&M) based on findings from security control assessments, security impact analyses, continuous monitoring of activities, audit reports, and other sources. When considering appropriate corrective actions to be taken, the agency should, to the extent possible, consider the potential agency-wide implications and design appropriate corrective actions to systemically address the deficiency.

NAS Incident Detection and Response Activities Were Limited

While FAA established POA&Ms for addressing identified security control weaknesses, it did not always complete remedial actions in accordance with established deadlines. For example, of the 147 POA&Ms we reviewed on 4 NAS systems, 58 were not completed by their planned completion dates, and the planned completion dates for 50 had been extended from between 8 months to more than 3 years past the dates that they were originally scheduled to be completed. According to ATO officials, one reason that original deadlines are often missed is that the programs lack sufficient resources and funding to address weaknesses by their original due dates. Without resolving identified vulnerabilities in a timely manner, FAA faces an increased risk, as continuing opportunities exist for unauthorized individuals to exploit these weaknesses and gain access to sensitive information and systems.

Comprehensive monitoring and incident response controls are necessary for rapidly detecting incidents, minimizing loss and destruction, mitigating the weaknesses that were exploited, and restoring computing services. While strong controls may not prevent all incidents, agencies can reduce the risks associated with these events by detecting and promptly responding before significant damage is done. NIST Special Publication 800-53 recommends that agencies test incident response capabilities for effectiveness. NIST guidance also notes that the ability to identify incidents using appropriate audit and monitoring techniques enables an agency to initiate its incident response plan in a timely manner. Further, NIST guidance also recommends that once an incident has been identified, an agency's incident response processes and procedures should provide the capability to correctly log the incident, properly analyze it, and take appropriate action. NIST guidance also recommends that agencies test their information technology plans, including incident response plans, and document the test results in an after action report. FAA's ATO assigned responsibility for incident handling on NAS systems to NCO, although NAS system owners and operators also have a responsibility to coordinate with NCO in responding to incidents affecting their systems.

FAA has notable shortcomings in security monitoring and incident detection over air traffic control systems. For example:

- NCO does not have sufficient access to effectively monitor the NAS operational environment. For example, there was no full network packet capture and anomaly detection capability for network traffic at major network interface points at FAA operational facilities. Additionally, network traffic flow session data was not integrated into the ad-hoc query systems used by the NCO. Further, NCO lacked access to data from sensors on key network gateways, including intrusion detection, network packet capture, and network flow data, and so cannot adequately monitor the gateways for security-relevant events.

- Although NCO has been given responsibility for incident response for the NAS environment, 26 of the 35 IP-connected NAS systems did not provide security event logs to NCO, including 3 of the systems we reviewed, severely limiting the ability of NCO to effectively monitor the NAS environment.
- The NCO database system containing centralized security logs collected from various NAS systems was ineffective due to weaknesses in its searching function. Specifically, the system could not search past any gaps in the log data. To compensate, NCO personnel would manually parse the data from multiple queries together, but there was not sufficient assurance that all data needed for incident investigations had been retrieved.
- NCO did not have a formal process in place to review and document the potential impact to NAS operations from significant incidents identified internally or by FAA's Cyber Security Management Center. Specifically, NCO did not formally assess the potential risks to the NAS for any of the incidents we reviewed.
- Testing of the NAS incident response capability has been limited. Specifically, while one system had conducted and documented tests of its incident response capability, NCO has not developed after-action reports for all phases of its incident response capability tests, and officials with three systems all indicated they do not test their incident response capabilities.

As a result, there is an increased risk that FAA will not be able to adequately detect, contain, eradicate, or recover from incidents affecting air traffic control systems.

Contingency Plans Were Not Always Complete or Adequately Tested

Losing the capability to process, retrieve, and protect electronically maintained information can significantly affect an agency's ability to accomplish its mission. If contingency planning controls are inadequate, even relatively minor interruptions can result in lost or incorrectly processed data, which can cause financial losses, expensive recovery efforts, and inaccurate or incomplete information. NIST Special Publication 800-34[24] recommends that contingency plans include procedures for diagnosing and addressing problems, notifying recovery personnel when the plan needs to be activated, and procedures to be followed in the event that specific personnel cannot be contacted. NIST also recommends that contingency plans include procedures for notifying users when a system has been reconstituted and normal operations have resumed. Additionally, NIST Special Publication 800-53 notes that contingency plans should be tested to determine the plan's effectiveness and the organization's readiness to execute the plan.

FAA did not always ensure that contingency plans for air traffic control systems were complete or that tests of the plans were adequate. Although FAA documented contingency plans for three systems, it did not always include important information in these plans. For example, the contingency plans for two systems did not sufficiently document the means by which key personnel were to be contacted in the event of a disaster or define procedures to follow in the event that specific personnel could not be contacted. Although separate notification procedures were developed for one of the systems, they were not included in the contingency plan either explicitly or by reference. Also, although procedures had been established for notifying users when two of the systems had been reconstituted and normal operations had resumed, the contingency plans for those systems did not include or reference the procedures. Further, the contingency plan for another system did not contain the actual assessment and recovery procedures for the system. Also, FAA tested the contingency plans for three NAS systems, but the tests did not always address key elements of the plans, including notification procedures, recovering the system on an alternate platform, and system performance on alternate equipment.

Without including important information in its contingency plans for air traffic control systems or sufficiently testing its contingency plans, FAA is at an increased risk of employees or contractors not following the correct procedures to appropriately recover systems in a timely manner from service disruptions.

Inadequate Agency-Wide Information Security Risk Management Processes Contribute to Weaknesses in Security Controls and Security Management

One important reason for many of the weaknesses in security controls as well as the security program shortcomings identified in our review is that FAA has not yet fully established an integrated, organization-wide approach to managing information security risk. According to NIST, effective risk management requires organizations such as the FAA to operate in highly complex, interconnected environments using state-of-the-art and legacy information systems—systems that organizations depend on to accomplish their missions and to conduct important business-related functions. The complex relationships among missions, mission/business processes, and the information systems supporting those missions and processes require an integrated, organization-wide view for managing risk. Effective management of information security risk is also critical to the success of organizations in achieving their strategic goals and objectives.

FISMA requires the head of each federal agency to ensure that information security management processes are integrated with agency strategic and operational planning processes. NIST SP 800-39 provides agencies with guidance for developing and implementing an integrated, organization-wide program for managing information security risk to agency operations (i.e., mission, functions, image, and reputation), organizational assets, individuals, other organizations, and the nation resulting from the operation and use of federal information systems. It describes an integrated approach for addressing information security risk at the organization level, the mission/business process level, and the information system level. NIST SP 800-39 states that, in managing information security risk at the organizational level, agencies should establish and implement information security governance, a risk executive function, and risk management strategy in order to ensure that risk management decisions are aligned strategically with the agency's missions and business functions consistent with the organizational goals and objectives. The publication also states that an organization's mission/business processes should be designed to manage risk in accordance with the organizational information security risk management strategy.

Further, NIST SP 800-100 notes that agencies should have a strategic plan for information security, which identifies goals and objectives related to the agency's mission, specifies a plan for achieving those goals, and establishes short- and mid-term performance targets and measures that allow the agency to track manage and monitor its progress towards those goals and objectives. Also, in February 2014, NIST established its *Framework for Improving Critical Infrastructure Cybersecurity*, which presents a set of industry standards and best practices to help organizations manage cybersecurity risks to critical infrastructure systems, and contains a methodology for organizations to evaluate and strengthen information security programs for critical infrastructure.

While it has taken initial steps, the FAA has not yet implemented an effective, organization-wide program for managing information security risk to its mission and operations. Specifically, the FAA Chief Information Security Officer stated that in November 2013, the agency established a risk executive function at the agency level in the form of a Cyber Security Steering Committee. The committee includes representatives from across FAA, including ATO, NextGen, and FAA's office of security. However, FAA has not yet fully established the governance structures and practices necessary for ensuring that its information security risk management decisions are aligned strategically with its mission. Specifically:

FAA has not clearly and consistently established roles and responsibilities for information security for NAS systems. FISMA requires the head of an agency to (1) ensure that senior agency officials provide security for information and information systems that support operations and assets under their control, and (2) delegate to the agency CIO the authority to ensure compliance with FISMA requirements. Further, according to NIST Special Publication 800-39, one of the tasks of the risk executive is to establish risk management roles and responsibilities. However, existing FAA practices, policies, and documentation are inconsistent in establishing responsibility for NAS information security. While FAA's security management program policy states that primary responsibility for NAS information security rests with the CIO, ATO officials stated that primary responsibility for NAS information security lies with ATO rather than the CIO. FAA's portion of the President's Fiscal Year 2014 Budget Submission states only that the CIO is responsible for non-NAS systems. The steering committee has defined updated roles and responsibilities for information security, which state that executive-level responsibility for the organization-wide information security program lies with the CIO. However, these roles and responsibilities have not yet been implemented. Additionally, AIT officials and ATO officials disagreed about whether the roles and responsibilities had been approved.

Better defining roles and responsibilities is important because FAA officials in AIT and ATO expressed diverging opinions about how information security controls should be implemented in the NAS environment. For example, AIT officials stated that ATO and AIT should collaborate to identify and reduce duplicative incident response activities between NCO and FAA's existing Cyber Security Management Center, but ATO officials stated that the NCO capability should remain separate from the Cyber Security Management Center because of the unique security requirements of the NAS critical infrastructure.

FAA does not have a strategic plan for information security that is up to date and reflects current conditions. FAA's Information Systems Security Program Policy requires a multiyear information security strategic plan to be developed, maintained, and updated annually. Additionally, NIST SP 800-100 states that agencies should revisit the information security strategic plan when a major change in the agency information security environment occurs. However, the FAA information security strategic plan has not been updated since 2010. Significant changes in the NAS environment, such as the increased reliance on IP networks, increased connectivity between systems, the introduction of NextGen systems, and the designation of the NAS as part of the nation's critical infrastructure, have changed the level and nature of the information security risks facing air traffic control systems. The evolution of connectivity for NAS systems substantially increases risks of Internet-based intrusions and disruptions. AIT officials told us that the Cyber Security Steering Committee plans to revise the information security strategic plan during fiscal year 2015.

Because FAA lacks an up-to-date information security strategic plan, the ATO organization does not have a clear set of goals, objectives, and performance measures around which it can organize its information security program. Responsibility for NAS information security in ATO is distributed across different entities and programs, and ATO officials stated that variation in emphasis on security goals and priorities across the organization makes it challenging to manage information security activities in the NAS environment. For example, according to ATO officials, the NAS incident response organization, NCO, has limited capabilities and available staff because it is required to obtain funding from other program units within ATO, which have different priorities. Additionally, ATO officials stated that remedial actions are often delayed because the program units do not hold system owners accountable for addressing information security weaknesses in a timely manner.

In the absence of clearly defined roles and responsibilities or an updated strategic plan, ATO has begun moving forward with strategic planning activities separately from the steering committee's risk management responsibilities. During our review, ATO evaluated its information security processes and capabilities against the guidance in the *NIST Framework for Improving Critical Infrastructure Cybersecurity*, with plans to use the results of the evaluation to develop an information security strategic plan for ATO. However, other organizations represented on the steering committee are not involved in this process. Although ATO officials told us that they plan to inform the members of the committee about the results of the review, it is not clear whether the committee intends to use the results in its efforts, or whether ATO's planned information security strategic plan will reflect the priorities of FAA as a whole.

Until it fully establishes an integrated, organization-wide approach to managing information security risk and ensures that federal guidance for securing critical infrastructure is incorporated into its risk management processes, FAA is likely to continue to face challenges in ensuring that risk management decisions are aligned strategically with the its mission and effectively implementing information security controls for air traffic control systems. As a result, the weaknesses we identified are likely to persist.

CONCLUSION

A large, complex, interconnected system like the NAS inherently faces many security risks. Although FAA took many steps to address these risks, weaknesses remain that challenge the FAA in fulfilling its mission of ensuring the safety and efficiency of the nation's airspace operations. Many weaknesses in access controls and configuration management pose risks to the security of the NAS. The effect of these weaknesses is increased by the significant interconnectivity that exists between the FTI NAS operational environment and the FTI mission support network. Additionally, significant shortcomings limit NCO's ability to detect and respond to security incidents across NAS systems. These weak controls are mirrored in weak security management processes, such as incomplete policies and procedures for incident response and insufficient testing of security controls. Additionally, actions to mitigate identified security weaknesses are often delayed—sometimes for years. All of these weaknesses combine to pose increased risks to the confidentiality, integrity, and availability of NAS systems and thus put the safe and uninterrupted operation of the nation's air traffic control system at risk.

A fundamental cause for these various weaknesses is that FAA has not yet implemented an effective program for managing organizational information security risk to its mission. Although FAA established a cyber security steering committee, roles and responsibilities remain unclear, and AIT and ATO officials continue to disagree on who should be responsible for the security of NAS systems. Likewise, an out-of-date information security strategic plan contributes to the lack of an adequate risk-based structure to guide implementation of security controls. Further, due in part to the lack of an up-to-date strategic plan for the agency, ATO lacks a clear set of goals, objectives, and performance measures around which it can organize its information security program for NAS systems, making it challenging to manage information security activities such as ensuring that controls are effectively implemented and that system owners address identified security weaknesses in a timely manner.

Until FAA establishes stronger agency-wide information security risk management processes, fully develops its NAS information security program, and ensures that remedial actions are addressed in a timely manner, the weaknesses that we identified are likely to continue, placing the safe and uninterrupted operation of the nation's air traffic control system at increased and unnecessary risk.

RECOMMENDATIONS FOR EXECUTIVE ACTION

To fully implement its information security program and ensure that unnecessary risks to the security of NAS systems are mitigated, we recommend that the Secretary of Transportation direct the Administrator of FAA to implement the following 14 recommendations:

- Finalize the incident response policy for ATO and ensure that NAS system-level incident response policies specify incident reporting timeframes and the need for all incidents to be reported in accordance with FAA guidance.
- Establish a mechanism to ensure that all contractor staff complete annual security awareness training as required by federal law and FAA policy.
- Establish a mechanism to ensure that all staff with significant security responsibilities receive appropriate role-based training.

- Establish a mechanism to ensure that personnel with incident response roles and responsibilities take appropriate training, and that training records are retained.
- Take steps to ensure that testing of security controls is comprehensive enough to determine whether security controls are in place and operating effectively, by, for example, examining artifacts such as audit reports, change tickets, and approval documents.
- Take steps to ensure that identified corrective actions for security weaknesses are implemented within prescribed timeframes.
- Provide NCO with full network packet capture capability for analyzing network traffic and detecting anomalies at major network interface points at FAA operational facilities.
- Integrate network traffic flow data into NCO's ad-hoc query systems.
- Provide NCO with access to network sensors on key network gateways for reviewing intrusion detection, network traffic, and network session data.
- Provide NCO with security event log data for all IP-connected NAS systems.
- Address identified weaknesses in the search function of the NCO database event query system to eliminate the need for manual workarounds and ensure that all data relevant for security investigations can be retrieved.
- Develop a formal process for NCO to assess significant identified incidents for potential impact to NAS operations.
- Ensure that NAS incident response capabilities are adequately tested, and that test results are sufficiently documented.
- Ensure that contingency plans for NAS systems are sufficiently documented, and that tests of contingency plans address key elements of the contingency plans, including notification procedures, recovering the system on an alternate platform, and system performance on alternate equipment.

Further, to establish an integrated organization-wide approach to managing information security risk and to ensure that risk management decisions are aligned strategically with the FAA's mission, we recommend that the Secretary of Transportation direct the Administrator of FAA to take the following three actions:

- Clearly define organizational responsibilities for information security for NAS systems, and ensure that all relevant organizations, including AIT and ATO, are in agreement with them.
- Update the FAA information security strategic plan to reflect current conditions, including the increased reliance on IP networking and the designation of the NAS as one of the nation's critical infrastructures.
- Create an agency-wide commitment to strategic planning for information security by ensuring that planning activities are coordinated with all relevant organizations represented on the Cyber Security Steering Committee.

We are also making 168 recommendations to address 60 findings in a separate report with limited distribution. These recommendations consist of actions to implement and correct specific information security weaknesses related to access controls and configuration management.

AGENCY COMMENTS AND OUR EVALUATION

In written comments on a draft of this report, the Department of Transportation stated that FAA concurred with our recommendations. The department also stated that FAA recognizes the need to secure the NAS environment as part of the nation's critical infrastructure, and that FAA has taken several steps to improve NAS information security. Additionally, the department stated that FAA recognizes that mission assurance requires the integration of all agency cyber capabilities to support operations and is continuing its efforts to establish an integrated organization-wide approach to managing information security risk. We agree that these actions are important steps for FAA to take, and we also believe that addressing our recommendations will result in valuable improvements in information security over air traffic control systems.

Gregory C. Wilshusen
Director, Information Security Issues
Nabajyoti Barkakati Ph.D.
Director, Center for Technology and Engineering
Gerald L. Dillingham, Ph.D.
Director, Physical Infrastructure Issues

Appendix I: Objective, Scope, and Methodology

The objective of our review was to evaluate the extent to which the Federal Aviation Administration (FAA) has effectively implemented appropriate information security controls to protect the confidentiality, integrity, and availability of its existing air traffic control (ATC) systems.

To determine the effectiveness of the FAA's security controls, we gained an understanding of the overall National Airspace System (NAS) control environment and examined controls for the agency's systems and facilities. Specifically, we reviewed controls over the network infrastructure and systems that support the FAA's mission to provide the safest, most efficient aerospace system in the world. We performed our work at FAA headquarters in Washington, D.C. and other locations supporting key systems, specifically: the Air Traffic Control System Command Center in Warrenton, Virginia; the FAA's William J. Hughes Technical Center in Egg Harbor Township, New Jersey; and at contractor facilities in Herndon, Virginia; Egg Harbor Township, New Jersey; and Melbourne, Florida.

To select the information systems for our audit, we evaluated each NAS information system based on several factors, including its relative importance in supporting FAA's mission, expected lifetime, and how widely it is used. Further, we selected only systems that use Internet Protocol (IP)-based communications. Based on this evaluation, we selected a non-generalizable sample of five systems[1] for review: FAA Telecommunications Infrastructure (FTI), Surveillance and Broadcast Service System (SBSS), Traffic Flow Management-Infrastructure (TFM-I), En Route Automation Modernization (ERAM), and En Route Communications Gateway (ECG).

To evaluate FAA's controls over its ATC systems, we used our *Federal Information System Controls Audit Manual*, [2] which contains guidance for reviewing information system controls that affect the confidentiality, integrity, and availability of computerized information; National Institute of Standards and Technology (NIST) standards and guidelines; FAA policies and procedures; and standards and guidelines from relevant security and IT security organizations, such as the National Security Agency and the Center for Internet Security. Specifically, we

- reviewed network access paths to determine if boundaries had been adequately protected;

- reviewed the complexity and expiration of password settings to determine if password management was being enforced;
- analyzed users' access authorizations for four systems to determine whether system access had been approved and properly documented;
- observed configurations for transmitting data across the network to determine whether sensitive data were being encrypted. For the ERAM and ECG systems, we reviewed configuration settings for network devices by reviewing the network device builds that are distributed to Air Route Traffic Control Centers (ARTCC) by the William J. Hughes Technical Center;
- reviewed system security settings to determine if sufficient audit and monitoring controls had been implemented;
- evaluated configuration change control processes for selected systems to determine whether changes were sufficiently documented, tested, and approved in accordance with system procedures; and
- inspected key network devices and servers to determine if critical patches had been installed and/or were up to date.

Additionally, our review of boundary protection controls focused on interconnections between NAS and non-NAS systems.

Using the requirements identified by the Federal Information Security Management Act of 2002, which establishes key elements for an effective agency-wide information security program, and associated NIST guidelines and agency requirements, we evaluated the FAA's information security program by

- analyzing processes and documentation that were part of FAA's information security risk management processes to determine the extent to which the process sufficiently supported the agency's mission and operations;
- examining system security plans to determine whether they described the security controls in place or planned for meeting the security requirements of the system;
- examining security awareness training records to determine whether employees and contractors had received training according to FAA policy and federal guidance;
- analyzing security testing and evaluation results for four systems to determine whether testing of management, operational, and technical

controls was sufficient to conclude that controls were in place and operating effectively;

- examining remedial action plans for four systems to determine whether FAA addressed identified vulnerabilities in a timely manner;
- examining contingency plans and contingency test results for selected systems to determine whether those plans were appropriately documented and had been sufficiently tested; and
- reviewing FAA's processes for identifying and responding to information security incidents to determine whether FAA has implemented an effective incident response capability for its air traffic control systems.

As part of our review of the FAA's information security program, we reviewed several sources of computer-generated data. These included FAA's

- inventory of NAS information systems,
- IT security training completion data, and
- employee background investigation data.

To verify the reliability of these data, we examined them for obvious outliers, omissions, errors, and consulted with FAA officials to resolve any identified anomalies. We also interviewed knowledgeable officials regarding controls on the security training and employee background investigation data, including how and by whom it is input and used. We determined that these sources of data were sufficiently reliable for our purposes.

We conducted this performance audit from August 2013 to January 2015 in accordance with generally accepted government auditing standards. Those standards require that we plan and perform the audit to obtain sufficient, appropriate evidence to provide a reasonable basis for our findings and conclusions based on our audit objectives. We believe that the evidence obtained provides a reasonable basis for our findings and conclusions based on our audit objective.

End Notes

[1] The USA PATRIOT Act of 2001 (42 U.S.C. § 5195c(e)) defines critical infrastructure as systems and assets, whether physical or virtual, so vital to our nation that their incapacity or destruction would have a debilitating impact on security, national economic security, national public health or safety, or any combination of these.

[2] The transportation systems sector (which includes aviation as a subsector) is 1 of 16 critical infrastructure sectors identified by Presidential Policy Directive 21 (PPD-21). The other sectors are chemical; commercial facilities; communications; critical manufacturing; dams; defense industrial base; emergency services; energy; financial services; food and agriculture; government facilities; healthcare and public health; information technology; nuclear reactors, materials, and waste; and water and wastewater systems

[3] These objectives typically include establishing/extending footholds within the information technology infrastructure of the targeted organizations for purposes of exfiltrating information; undermining or impeding critical aspects of a mission, program, or organization; or establishing the capability to carry out these objectives in the future. An advanced persistent threat (1) pursues its objectives repeatedly over an extended period of time, (2) adapts to defenders' efforts to resist it, and (3) is determined to maintain the level of interaction needed to achieve its objectives.

[4] We currently have a separate review underway examining FAA's integration of information security requirements in its acquisition of NextGen programs. We plan to issue a report on that review later in 2015.

[5] GAO, High-Risk Series: Information Management and Technology, GAO/HR-97-9 (Washington, D.C.: Feb. 1, 1997).

[6] See, most recently, GAO, High-Risk Series: An Update, GAO-13-283 (Washington, D.C.: Feb. 14, 2013).

[7] NIST, Framework for Improving Critical Infrastructure Cybersecurity, Version 1.0 (Gaithersburg, Md.: Feb. 12, 2014).

[8] FISMA was enacted as title III, E-Government Act of 2002, Pub. L. No. 107-347, 116 Stat. 2899, 2946 (Dec. 17, 2002). As our review was finishing, the Federal Information Security Modernization Act of 2014 (Pub. L. No. 113-283, Dec. 18, 2014) was enacted. However, the new law, which supersedes FISMA, incorporates the requirements from FISMA that we relied upon in our report. Accordingly, no changes to our findings were necessary.

[9] NIST, Standards for Security Categorization of Federal Information and Information Systems, FIPS Publication 199 (Gaithersburg, Md.: February 2004).

[10] NIST, Minimum Security Requirements for Federal Information and Information Systems, FIPS Publication 200 (Gaithersburg, Md.: March 2006).

[11] NIST, Contingency Planning Guide for Federal Information Systems, SP 800-34, Revision 1 (Gaithersburg, Md.: May 2010).

[12] NIST, Guide for Applying the Risk Management Framework to Federal Information Systems: A Security Life Cycle Approach, SP 800-37, Revision 1 (Gaithersburg, Md.: February 2010).

[13] NIST, Managing Information Security Risk: Organization, Mission, and Information System View, SP 800-39 (Gaithersburg, Md.: March 2011).

[14] NIST, Security and Privacy Controls for Federal Information Systems and Organizations, SP 800-53, Revision 4 (Gaithersburg, Md.: April 2013).

[15] NIST, Guide to Industrial Control Systems (ICS) Security, SP 800-82 (Gaithersburg, Md.: May 2013).

[16] NIST, Information Security Handbook: A Guide for Managers, SP 800-100 (Gaithersburg, Md.: October 2006).

[17] NIST, SP 800-53.

[18] FAA policy permits passwords of 13 or more random, non-sequential characters to never expire, and requires them to be changed only in the event they are compromised. The policy states this is permitted based on research suggesting the time required to crack such a password makes such an attack impractical.

[19] Users should have the least amount of privileges (access to services) necessary to perform their duties.

[20] NIST, Guide for Security-Focused Configuration Management of Information Systems, SP 800-128 (Gaithersburg, Md.: August 2011).

[21] NIST, SP 800-53.

[22] FAA officials were unable to tell us when the policy would be finalized.

[23] NIST, Guide for Assessing the Security Controls in Federal Information Systems and Organizations, SP 800-53A, Revision 1 (Gaithersburg, Md.: June 2010).

[24] NIST, SP 800-34.

End Notes for Appendix I

[1] Because we examined only 5 of the more than 100 air traffic control systems in the NAS, the results of our review of system-level controls cannot be generalized to the entire NAS environment.

[2] GAO, Federal Information System Controls Audit Manual (FISCAM), GAO-09-232G (Washington, D.C.: February 2009).

In: Information Security and Cybersecurity ... ISBN: 978-1-63483-312-7
Editor: Victor Morris

Chapter 2

AIR TRAFFIC CONTROL: FAA NEEDS A MORE COMPREHENSIVE APPROACH TO ADDRESS CYBERSECURITY AS AGENCY TRANSITIONS TO NEXTGEN*

United States Government Accountability Office

WHY GAO DID THIS STUDY

FAA is responsible for overseeing the national airspace system, which comprises ATC systems, procedures, facilities, and aircraft, and the people who operate them. FAA is implementing NextGen to move the current radar-based ATC system to one that is based on satellite navigation and automation. It is essential that FAA ensures effective information-security controls are incorporated in the design of NextGen programs to protect them from threats.

GAO was asked to review FAA's cybersecurity efforts. This report (1) identifies the cybersecurity challenges facing FAA as it shifts to the NextGen ATC system and how FAA has begun addressing those challenges, and (2) assesses the extent to which FAA and its contractors, in the acquisition of NextGen programs, have followed federal guidelines for incorporating cybersecurity controls. GAO reviewed FAA cybersecurity policies and

* This is an edited, reformatted and augmented version of a United States Government Accountability Office publication, No. GAO-15-370, dated April 2015.

procedures and federal guidelines, and interviewed FAA officials, aviation industry stakeholders, and 15 select cybersecurity experts based on their work and recommendations by other experts.

What GAO Recommends

GAO recommends that FAA: 1) assess developing a cybersecurity threat model, 2) include AVS as a full member of the Committee, and 3) develop a plan to implement NIST revisions within OMB's time frames. FAA concurred with recommendations one and three, but believes that AVS is sufficiently involved in cybersecurity. GAO maintains that AVS should be a member of the Committee.

What GAO Found

As the agency transitions to the Next Generation Air Transportation System (NextGen), the Federal Aviation Administration (FAA) faces cybersecurity challenges in at least three areas: (1) protecting air-traffic control (ATC) information systems, (2) protecting aircraft avionics used to operate and guide aircraft, and (3) clarifying cybersecurity roles and responsibilities among multiple FAA offices.

- As GAO reported in January 2015, FAA has taken steps to protect its ATC systems from cyber-based threats; however, significant security-control weaknesses remain that threaten the agency's ability to ensure the safe and uninterrupted operation of the national airspace system. FAA has agreed to address these weaknesses. Nevertheless, FAA will continue to be challenged in protecting ATC systems because it has not developed a cybersecurity threat model. NIST guidance, as well as experts GAO consulted, recommend such modeling to identify potential threats to information systems, and as a basis for aligning cybersecurity efforts and limited resources. While FAA has taken some steps toward developing such a model, it has no plans to produce one and has not assessed the funding or time that would be needed to do so. Without such a model, FAA may not be allocating resources properly to guard against the most significant cybersecurity threats.

- Modern aircraft are increasingly connected to the Internet. This interconnectedness can potentially provide unauthorized remote access to aircraft avionics systems. As part of the aircraft certification process, FAA's Office of Safety (AVS) currently certifies new interconnected systems through rules for specific aircraft and has started reviewing rules for certifying the cybersecurity of all new aircraft systems.
- FAA is making strides to address the challenge of clarifying cybersecurity roles and responsibilities among multiple FAA offices, such as creating a Cyber Security Steering Committee (the Committee) to oversee information security. However, AVS is not represented on the Committee but can be included on an ad-hoc advisory basis. Not including AVS as a full member could hinder FAA's efforts to develop a coordinated, holistic, agency-wide approach to cybersecurity.

FAA's acquisition management process generally aligned with federal guidelines for incorporating requirements for cybersecurity controls in its acquisition of NextGen programs. For example, the process included the six major information-technology and risk-management activities as described by NIST. Timely implementation of some of these activities could have been improved based on their importance to NextGen, cost, and deployment status. The Surveillance and Broadcast Services Subsystem (SBSS)—which enables satellite guidance of aircraft and is currently deployed in parts of the nation—has not adopted all of the April 2013 changes to NIST security controls, such as intrusion detection improvements, although the Office of Management and Budget guidance states that deployed systems must adopt changes within one year. Systems with weaknesses that could be exploited by adversaries may be at increased risk if relevant controls are not implemented.

ABBREVIATIONS

ADS-B	Automatic Dependent Surveillance—Broadcast
AMS	Acquisition Management System
ARAC	Aviation Rulemaking Advisory Committee
ASISP	aircraft system's information security/protection

ATC	air traffic control
ATO	Air Traffic Organization
AVS	Office of Safety
CATM	Collaborative Air Traffic Management
CDM	*Continuous Diagnostics and Mitigation*
CIO	Chief Information Officer
CISO	Chief Information Security Officer
CSC	Cybersecurity Steering Committee
CSMC	Cyber Security Management Center
CSS-Wx	Common Support Services—Weather
Data Comm	Data Communications
DHS	Department of Homeland Security
FAA	Federal Aviation Administration
FISMA	Federal Information Security Management Act of 2002
GPS	Global Positioning System
IP	Internet Protocol
ISS	Information Systems Security
IT	information technology
NAS	national airspace system
NCO	NAS Cyber Operations Center
NextGen	Next Generation Air Transportation System
NIST	National Institute of Standards and Technology
NVS	NAS Voice Switch
OMB	Office of Management and Budget
POA&M	plans of action and milestones
RTCA	Radio Technical Commission for Aeronautics
SBSS	Surveillance and Broadcast Services Subsystem
SWIM	System Wide Information Management
US-CERT	United States Computer Emergency Readiness Team
WBS	work breakdown structure

* * *

April 14, 2015

Congressional Requesters

Cyber-based threats to federal information systems are evolving and growing. These threats can come from many sources, including criminals and other adversarial groups, foreign nations, terrorists, and insiders. Further, the growing interconnectivity among information systems presents increasing opportunities for cyber attacks. Specifically, the number of incidents reported by federal agencies to the United States Computer Emergency Readiness Team[1] (US-CERT) has increased dramatically in recent years from 5,503 incidents reported in fiscal year 2006 to 60,753 incidents in fiscal year 2013. Federal policy identifies 16 infrastructure sectors critical to the nation's security, economy, and public health and safety[2]—including the nation's air-traffic-control and federal-information technology systems—that rely extensively on computerized information systems and electronic data. Effectively implementing appropriate security over the information systems and data can make these sectors more resilient to attack or unintentional compromise.

For more than 10 years, the Federal Aviation Administration (FAA) has been modernizing the air-traffic control (ATC) system across the national airspace system (NAS). FAA initiated its current modernization efforts in 2004 with the Next Generation Air Transportation System (NextGen), which consists of several programs that provide digital communications between controllers and pilots, as well as between satellite-based surveillance and navigation. NextGen increases reliance on integrated information systems and distribution of information, digital communication methods, and Global Positioning System (GPS) technology that may put the ATC system at greater risk for intentional or unintentional information-system failures and breaches. You asked us to examine these risks. This report identifies the cybersecurity challenges facing FAA as it shifts to the NextGen ATC system and how FAA has begun addressing those challenges. In addition, this report assesses the extent to which FAA and its contractors, in the acquisition of NextGen programs, have followed federal guidelines for incorporating cybersecurity controls.

To ascertain the key challenges FAA faces and how it is addressing them, we reviewed relevant cybersecurity documents from FAA and asked FAA officials to provide us with detailed descriptions of their cybersecurity plans as they relate to the NextGen ATC system. We interviewed FAA officials in the Air Traffic Organization—specifically the Technical Operations Information Security Office, NAS Cyber Operations Center, and the Program Management Office; the Office of NextGen; the Office of Safety; and the Office of Finance and Management—to identify information about the cybersecurity risks and challenges officials have identified, as well as mitigation strategies either in place or planned. We interviewed a diverse but non-generalizable sample of 15 aviation and cybersecurity experts in private industry and academia to obtain their views on FAA's efforts to address NextGen cybersecurity issues. We selected these experts based on their knowledge of these topics, as demonstrated by their publications, participation as experts in prior relevant GAO work, or recommendation by other experts. We also reviewed studies on NextGen cybersecurity challenges and spoke with a variety of industry stakeholders and academics.

To assess the extent to which FAA and its contractors, in the acquisition of NextGen programs, have followed federal guidelines for incorporating cybersecurity controls, we compared pertinent FAA policies, procedures, and practices with selected federal information-security laws and federal guidance, including standards and guidelines from the National Institute of Standards and Technology (NIST).[3] In particular, we compared FAA's Acquisition Management System (AMS)[4] against NIST's risk management guidelines[5] and information-technology security guidelines[6] to determine if it follows these guidelines for the six foundational NextGen programs, Surveillance and Broadcast Services Subsystem (SBSS), Data Communications (Data Comm), NAS Voice Switch, Collaborative Air Traffic Management (CATM), Common Support Service-Weather (CSSWx), and System Wide Information Management (SWIM). We analyzed FAA's documentation of key cybersecurity activities for these programs and interviewed program managers to determine if FAA completed the key activities in the process, or has plans to complete activities that were started but not completed. We then chose two key NextGen acquisitions, SBSS and Data Comm. We chose them for a detailed, in-depth review because of their importance to NextGen, their cost, and their deployment status. SBSS has completed key activities in the acquisition cycle. Our reviewing Data Comm, which has not completed the cycle, should allow insight into how the process has changed and what still might be an issue for upcoming programs. For these two programs, we assessed how well FAA and its contractors completed key cybersecurity activities and the extent to which they complied with AMS and NIST guidelines relating to cybersecurity. As part of this effort, we also compared documentation of program activities and plans to these requirements, and interviewed agency officials. We also reviewed pertinent sections of prior GAO reports related to cybersecurity. We performed our work at FAA headquarters in Washington, D.C.; the Air Traffic Control Systems Command Center in Warrenton, Virginia; and an FAA contractor location in Herndon, Virginia. See appendix I for a more detailed description of our scope and methodology.

We conducted this performance audit from September 2013 to March 2015, in accordance with generally accepted government auditing standards. Those standards require that we plan and perform the audit to obtain sufficient, appropriate evidence to provide a reasonable basis for our findings and conclusions based on our audit objectives. We believe that the evidence obtained provides a reasonable basis for our findings and conclusions based on our audit objectives.

BACKGROUND

FAA's Transition to NextGen

NextGen is a modernization effort begun in 2004 by FAA to transform the nation's ground-based ATC system into a system that uses satellite-based navigation and other advanced technology. This effort is a multiyear, incremental transformation that will introduce new technologies and leverage existing technologies to affect every part of the NAS. These new technologies will use an Internet Protocol (IP) based network to communicate.[7] See figure 1 below for a graphic illustration of the different parts of the NAS, the flow of information among them, and their transition to an IP-based network.

According to FAA, the shift to NextGen technologies will require FAA to replace its proprietary, relatively isolated ATC computer systems with information systems that interoperate and share data throughout FAA's operations and those of its aviation partners. These combined aviation operations are known as *the enterprise*. These new systems, which will be described in detail later in this report, will use IP-networking technologies to communicate across the enterprise. This transformation involves acquiring, certifying, and operating a vast network of navigation, communications, and surveillance systems, including information systems in the cockpits of thousands of aircraft (avionics); it will also employ digital and Internet-based computer-networking technologies, exposing the air-traffic control (ATC) system to new cybersecurity risks.

NextGen comprises many programs that are in various stages of acquisition and deployment in the NAS. FAA classifies six programs as its foundational NextGen programs: Surveillance and Broadcast Services Subsystem (SBSS), Collaborative Air Traffic Management (CATM), Common Support Services Weather (CSS-Wx), Data Communications (Data Comm),

NAS Voice Switch (NVS), and System Wide Information Management (SWIM) (see fig. 2).

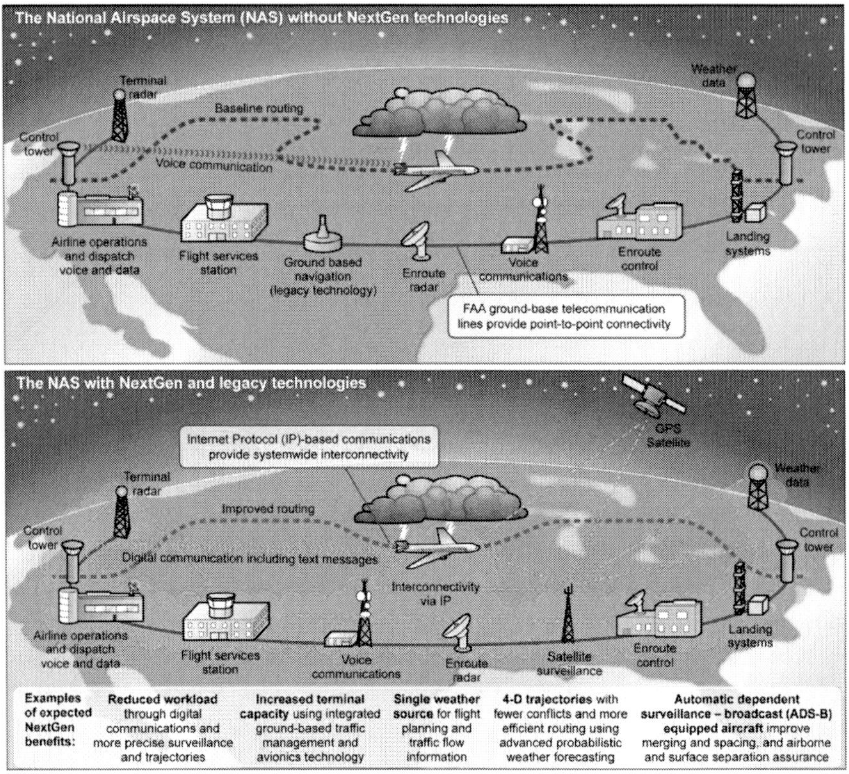

Source: GAO. | GAO-15-370.

Figure 1. National Airspace System's Transition to an IP Network.

For the six programs we examined, FAA relies on contractors to assist with or complete most of the broad information technology and risk management activities. NIST, OMB, and FISMA state that regardless of whether a security task was performed by a contractor or by a federal agency, the federal agency is ultimately responsible for ensuring system security. The AMS requires that FAA program officials monitor the contractors' performance in implementing contractual requirements, including those related to security.

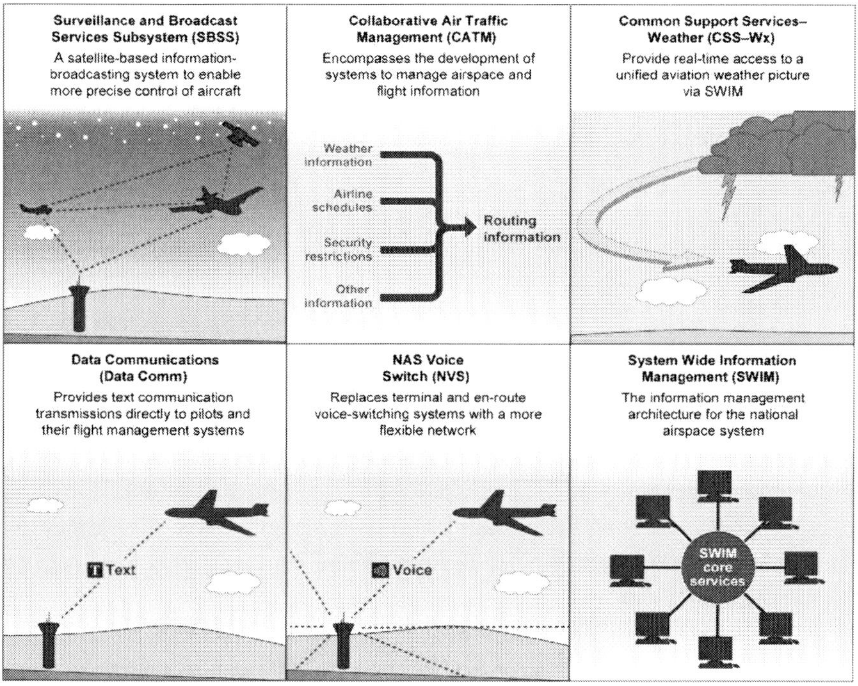

Source: GAO. I GAO-15-370.

Figure 2. NextGen Foundational Programs.

Several Offices within FAA Have Cybersecurity Responsibilities

- The Office of the Chief Information Security Officer within the Office of Finance and Management oversees cybersecurity across the three main areas of FAA activity known as *domains* (i.e., NAS ATC operations, Mission Support, and Research and Development [R&D]). This office provides operational security services to the Mission Support and R&D domains through efforts across FAA, as well as the Cyber Security Management Center (CSMC). The CSMC provides system monitoring and vulnerability remediation for FAA's standard information-technology systems that support the agency. Mission-support information systems, such as email, are separate from the NAS and R&D domain systems.[8]
- The Air Traffic Organization (ATO), the operational arm of FAA, implements and oversees cybersecurity measures for ATC

information systems through several of its offices.[9] The ATO's NAS Security Risk Executive (Risk Executive) located in Technical Operations has responsibility for cybersecurity on all NAS ATC systems, including continuous monitoring, threat response coordination, and policy.[10] According to FAA, the Risk Executive works internally with FAA's Security and Hazardous Materials Office and NextGen offices, and externally with Department of Homeland Security (DHS) and airline stakeholders to provide an understanding of FAA's critical mission and how it relates to other critical infrastructures. Another office within ATO, the NAS Cyber Operations unit, is responsible for monitoring some NAS systems, network data flows, and cyber events to detect anomalous and unauthorized cyber activities in the NAS domain. ATO's Program Management Office is responsible for developing and fulfilling cybersecurity and all other system requirements for NAS information systems, including NextGen systems, through the acquisitions process.

- The Office of NextGen develops and disseminates cybersecurity policy on NextGen's system engineering and controls, develops the NAS Enterprise Architecture, which is the agency's long-term strategic plan for NextGen that includes, among other things, the information systems security (ISS) plans, and is responsible for the overall implementation of FAA's NextGen initiative.
- The Office of Security and Hazardous Material Safety performs internal forensics investigations on computers that CSMC identifies as involved in activity that may compromise cybersecurity.
- The Office of Safety certifies the safety of all aircraft and aircraft equipment, including the software components for the avionics systems that could affect the safe operation of an aircraft.

Federal Cybersecurity Guidance for Information Systems

The Federal Information Security Management Act of 2002 (FISMA)[11] established a comprehensive framework to better ensure the effectiveness of security controls[12] over information resources that support federal operations and assets. FISMA[13] requires each agency to develop, document, and implement an agency-wide information-security program, using a risk-based approach to determine and address cybersecurity requirements for information system management. Such a program includes planning, implementing, evaluating, and documenting remedial actions to address information security deficiencies. Federal cybersecurity guidelines, such as those published by NIST, strongly encourage agencies to implement information cybersecurity early in the process of developing information systems. In this manner, the cybersecurity requirements can change as needed and be integrated cost-effectively.[14] NIST also provides a process for integrating information-security and risk-management activities into the system development process over the life of the system. Accordingly, NIST has developed a risk management framework of standards and guidelines for agencies to follow in developing information security programs. Relevant publications include the following:

- *Guide for Applying the Risk Management Framework to Federal Information Systems: A Security Life Cycle Approach* provides a process that integrates information-security and risk-management activities into the system development's life cycle including security categorization, security control selection and implementation, security control assessment, information system authorization, and security control monitoring of an information system.
- *Security and Privacy Controls for Federal Information Systems and Organizations*[15] provides a catalog of security and privacy controls for federal information systems and organizations, and a process for selecting controls to protect organizational operations, assets, individuals, other organizations, and the nation from a diverse set of threats including hostile cyber attacks, natural disasters, structural failures, and human errors. The guidance includes privacy controls to be used in conjunction with the specified security controls to achieve comprehensive security and privacy protection.
- *Security Considerations in the System Development Life Cycle*[16] presents a framework for incorporating security across the life cycle of a system and describes a minimum set of security steps needed to effectively incorporate security into a system during its development. It is intended to help agencies select and acquire cost-effective security controls by explaining how to include information-system security requirements in the system development's life cycle.
- In addition to these NIST publications, the Office of Management and Budget's (OMB) Security of Federal Automated Information Resources[17] establishes a minimum set of controls to be included in federal automated information-security programs; assigns federal

agency responsibilities for the security of automated information; and links the agency's automated information-security programs and the agency's management control systems.

FAA Acquisition Management System

FAA's Acquisition Management System (AMS) provides policies and guidance for managing all of its acquisitions. The AMS serves as the framework for IT project management and risk evaluation to help ensure that systems are developed and maintained on time and within budget, and that they deliver the capabilities necessary to meet user requirements including the development and integration of cybersecurity controls.

FAA's Shift to NextGen Implementation Raises Cybersecurity Challenges That FAA Has Taken Some Steps to Address

FAA faces cybersecurity challenges in at least three areas: (1) protecting its air traffic control (ATC) information systems, (2) securing aircraft avionics used to operate and guide aircraft, and (3) clarifying cybersecurity roles and responsibilities among multiple FAA offices. FAA has taken several steps to address these challenges, but cybersecurity experts suggested additional actions FAA could take to enhance cybersecurity.

FAA Faces Cybersecurity Challenges to Protect ATC Information Systems, and Most Experts Consulted Indicated That FAA Could Take Additional Steps

New Networking Technologies Expose ATC Systems to New Cybersecurity Risks

New networking technologies connecting FAA's ATC information systems expose these systems to new cybersecurity risks, potentially increasing opportunities for systems to be compromised and damaged. Such damage could stem both from attackers seeking to gain access to and move among information systems, and from trusted users of the systems, such as controllers or pilots, who might inadvertently cause harm. FAA's ATC-related information systems are currently a mixture of old, legacy systems and new, IP-networked systems. FAA's legacy systems consist mainly of decades-old, point-to-point, hardwired information systems, such as controller voice-switching systems, that share information only within their limited, wired configuration. In contrast, FAA plans for NextGen call for the new information systems to be networked together with IP technology into an overarching system of interoperating subsystems.

According to FAA officials and experts we consulted, the ease of access to these different types of systems, and the potential to damage them, varies. The older systems, depicted on the left in figure 3 below, are difficult to access remotely because few of them connect from FAA to external entities such as through the Internet. They also have limited lines of direct connection within FAA. Conversely, the new information systems for NextGen programs are designed to interoperate with other systems and use IP networking to communicate within FAA, as shown on the right in figure 3 below. According to experts, if one system connected to an IP network is compromised, damage can potentially spread to other systems on the network, continually expanding the parts of the system at risk. As shown in the figure, cybersecurity controls, if properly designed and effectively implemented, can make IP-networked systems more resilient against damage while allowing the systems to interoperate. According to MITRE,[18] because the older systems had limited connectivity, they were generally not protected with cybersecurity controls. Once one of them is breached, it is easy to potentially damage that system, gain access to other systems with which it communicates, and potentially damage those systems as well. According to FAA, so far, approximately 36 percent of the ATC systems in the national airspace system (NAS) are connected using IP, and FAA officials expect the percentage of NAS systems using IP networking to grow to 50 to 60 percent by 2020. According to MITRE and other experts, a hybrid system comprising both IP-connected and point-to-point subsystems increases the potential for the point-to-point systems to be compromised because of the increased connectivity to the system as a whole provided by the IP-connected systems.

We reported in January 2015 that FAA has taken steps to protect its ATC systems from cyber-based threats. However, we stated that significant security-control weaknesses remain that threaten the agency's ability to ensure the safe and uninterrupted operation of the national airspace system. We made numerous recommendations to address these weaknesses, and FAA has concurred with these recommendations.[19]

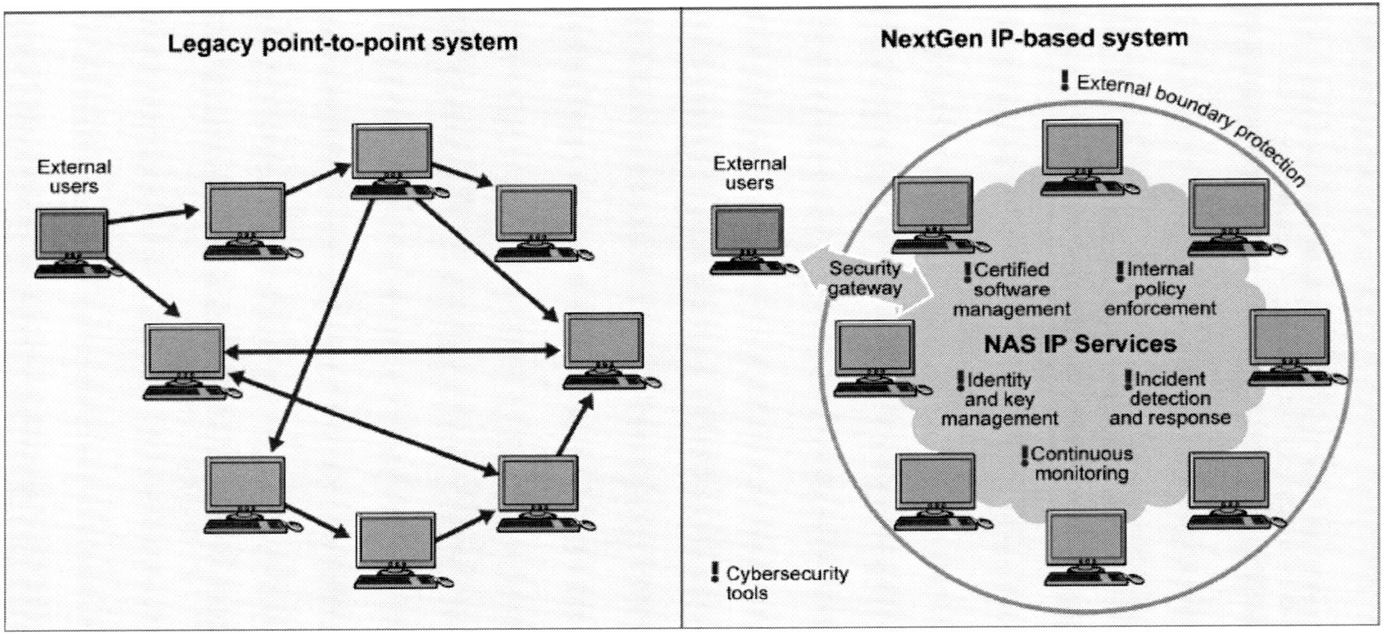

Source: GAO. | GAO-15-370.

Figure 3. Legacy NAS ATC Systems Compared to NAS IP Networks.

FAA Is Designing and Deploying an Enterprise Approach Intended to Strengthen the Cybersecurity of Its Information Systems

FAA is developing an approach, called an *enterprise* approach, to connect and protect its information systems enterprise-wide. The enterprise approach views IP-networked systems as subsystems within the larger enterprise-wide system. Under this approach, the subsystems can interoperate while an enterprise-wide set of shared cybersecurity controls,[20] called "*common controls*," and a monitoring program protect and increase the resiliency of the subsystems. According to FAA officials and cybersecurity experts we spoke to, using common controls in an enterprise approach increases the efficiency of cybersecurity efforts. For example, NIST recommends the use of common controls because when new threats to the system are discovered and those threats can be addressed by revisions to common controls, agencies can then immediately protect all the interoperating subsystems by revising just the common control. For isolated, legacy systems, cybersecurity control revisions have to be developed and implemented uniquely for each individual system. FAA officials said that they apply both common controls and individual system controls, where appropriate, to IPconnected systems interoperating within an enterprise domain, in accordance with NIST guidance and OMB policy.

Selected Experts Generally Agreed That FAA's Enterprise Approach Is Appropriate, but Noted That Further Actions Could Enhance Cybersecurity

A Holistic Threat Model Could Enhance FAA's Cybersecurity Posture

Twelve of our 15 cybersecurity experts discussed enterprise-level holistic threat modeling, and all 12 agreed that FAA should develop such a model to strengthen cybersecurity agency-wide. NIST and the 12 experts we consulted said that threat modeling, a cybersecurity best practice, enables an organization to identify known threats, including insider threats, across its organization and align its cybersecurity efforts and limited resources accordingly to protect its mission. NIST guidance also states that an integrated, agency-wide view for managing risk can address the complex relationship among missions, the business processes needed to carry out missions, and the information systems supporting those missions and processes. NIST also recommends organization-wide threat modeling,[21] assessment, and monitoring because an agency-wide threat model would help to identify all known threats to information systems, allowing an agency to further identify vulnerabilities in those systems.

FAA officials said that FAA has not produced a plan to develop an enterprise-wide threat model but has made some initial steps toward developing such a model. Specifically, FAA officials said that they have examined threats to the future NextGen air-transportation system and are currently working to develop multiple threat models. Such efforts include reviewing the resiliency of the ATC system in conjunction with the Department of Homeland Security (DHS). NIST recommended such a review in its guidelines to promote the protection of critical infrastructure. According to FAA, it also assesses risks associated with individual systems when it acquires them and during system reauthorization. According to FAA, these assessments examine how the system in question interoperates with other systems; however, FAA officials agree that these assessments do not constitute a holistic threat model that might give FAA an agency-wide view of known threats to the entire ATC system. One FAA official said and an aviation advisory group published a report stating that such a threat model would allow FAA to approach cybersecurity in a proactive way, whereas FAA's current activities are reactive. For example, a threat model like that recommended by NIST and our experts could help FAA be more proactive in dealing with the rise of insider threats in federal agencies.[22]

FAA officials told us that they have not yet reached a point where they are prepared to pursue a comprehensive enterprise-wide threat model. Some experts told us that developing and maintaining a threat model would be costly and time consuming. FAA officials told us that they have not determined the funding or time that would be needed to develop such a model or identified the resources needed to implement it. One senior FAA official agreed with the experts' view that an enterprise holistic-wide threat model is expensive and time-consuming to accomplish and maintain; he said that no plan currently exists to produce one for this reason.

While developing a holistic threat model could be costly and time-consuming, in a constrained-resource environment such as FAA's, the information contained in such a model could allow FAA to target resources to parts of the system commensurate with the likelihood of compromise and the danger associated with the potential consequences that might occur. Without a holistic threat model, it is unclear how FAA will be able to develop a more comprehensive picture of threats to its systems, and how they might compromise these systems. Most of our experts said that without this knowledge, FAA might not target its cybersecurity resources and analyses appropriately, leaving some important risks unmitigated while overprotecting against less severe risks.

Continuous-Monitoring Efforts Are under Way

Ten of the cybersecurity experts we contacted also said that a holistic continuous-monitoring program is necessary for the IP-networked agency-wide approach that FAA is taking to accommodate NextGen programs. Cybersecurity experts and FAA officials told us that a holistic, continuous-monitoring program includes (1) real-time monitoring of the enterprise system's boundaries, (2) detection of would-be attackers probing for vulnerabilities, (3) real-time monitoring and investigation of internal user activity that is outside expectations, and (4) other continuous-monitoring activities such as incident detection, response, and recovery activities and mitigations.

FAA officials said they have implemented some monitoring activities for ATC systems. Although no coordinated policy exists for FAA enterprise-wide continuous monitoring, the Cyber Security Steering Committee has developed a plan that will incorporate DHS's Continuous Diagnostics and Mitigation program[23] in the future. For example, the NAS Cyber Operations (NCO) group, which has responsibility for incident response for NAS ATC systems, daily analyzes ATC's system activity reports, which, among other things, report on cyber attacks. Currently 9 of 39 IP- connected ATC systems provide system activity reports for NCO's review. NCO does not currently analyze activity reports for the other 30 systems. We have previously found[24] that this limited monitoring ability increased the risk that a cybersecurity event affecting NAS systems could go undetected and recommended that FAA provide the NCO function with sufficient access to provide more comprehensive monitoring. FAA officials said that ATO plans to have all NAS's IP-connected systems reporting daily to NCO within 3 years.

Securing Aircraft Avionics Systems Is an Increasing Challenge as FAA Adapts Its Aircraft Certification Process to Better Focus on Cybersecurity

According to FAA and experts we interviewed, modern communications technologies, including IP connectivity, are increasingly used in aircraft systems, creating the possibility that unauthorized individuals might access and compromise aircraft avionics systems. Aircraft information systems consist of avionics systems used for flight and in-flight entertainment (see fig. 4 below). Historically, aircraft in flight and their avionics systems used for flight guidance and control functioned as isolated and self-contained units, which protected their avionics systems from remote attack. However, according to FAA and experts we spoke to, IP networking may allow an attacker to gain remote access to avionics systems and compromise them—as shown in figure 4 (below). Firewalls protect avionics systems located in the cockpit from intrusion by cabin-system users, such as passengers who use in-flight entertainment services onboard. Four cybersecurity experts with whom we spoke discussed firewall vulnerabilities, and all four said that because firewalls are software components, they could be hacked like any other software and circumvented. The experts said that if the cabin systems connect to the cockpit avionics systems (e.g., share the same physical wiring harness or router) and use the same networking platform, in this case IP, a user could subvert the firewall and access the cockpit avionics system from the cabin. An FAA official said that additional security controls implemented onboard could strengthen the system.

FAA officials and experts we interviewed said that modern aircraft are also increasingly connected to the Internet, which also uses IPnetworking technology and can potentially provide an attacker with remote access to aircraft information systems. According to cybersecurity experts we interviewed, Internet connectivity in the cabin should be considered a direct link between the aircraft and the outside world, which includes potential malicious actors. FAA officials and cybersecurity and aviation experts we spoke to said that increasingly passengers in the cabin can access the Internet via onboard wireless broadband systems. One cybersecurity expert noted that a virus or malware planted in websites visited by passengers could provide an opportunity for a malicious attacker to access the IP-connected onboard information system through their infected machines. According to five cybersecurity experts, the threat of malicious activity by trusted insiders also grows with the ease of access to avionics systems afforded by IP connectivity if proper controls, such as *role-based* access,[25] are not in place. For example, the presence of personal smart phones and tablets in the cockpit increases the risk of a system's being compromised by trusted insiders, both malicious and non-malicious, if these devices have the capability to transmit information to aircraft avionics systems.

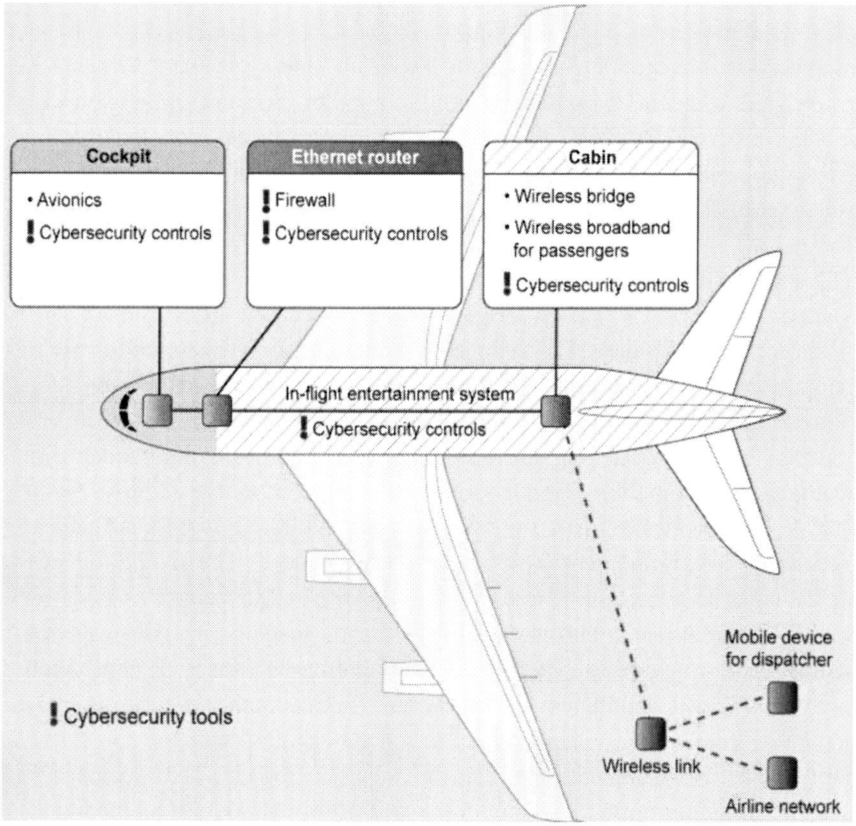

Source: GAO. I GAO-15-370.

Figure 4. Aircraft Diagram Showing Internet Protocol Connectivity Inside and Outside of Aircraft.

FAA's Office of Safety (AVS) is responsible for certifying the airworthiness of new aircraft and aviation equipment, including software components for avionics systems.[26] Although FAA's aircraft-airworthiness certification does not currently include assurance that cybersecurity is addressed,[27]

FAA currently issues rules with limited scope, called Special Conditions, to aircraft manufacturers when aircraft employ new technologies where IP interconnectivity could present cybersecurity risks. FAA views Special Conditions as an integral part of the certification process, which gives the manufacturer approval to design and manufacture the aircraft, engine, or propeller with additional capabilities not referred to in FAA regulations. For example, FAA issued Special Conditions to address the increased connectivity among aircraft cockpit and cabin systems for the Boeing 787 and Airbus A350 to provide systems cybersecurity and computer network protection from unauthorized external and internal access. FAA officials said that research supporting cybersecurity-related Special Conditions could be aggregated and used to support portions of a new rule, and industry experts we spoke with said they would support the certainty rulemaking would bring.

According to FAA officials and the Radio Technical Commission for Aeronautics (RTCA),[28] FAA has not yet developed new regulations to certify cybersecurity assurance for avionics systems because historically, aircraft avionics systems were isolated within the aircraft itself and not considered vulnerable to cybersecurity attacks. According to RTCA, FAA's certification process for component airworthiness focuses on design assurance, which evaluates the probability and consequences of component failure. Further, RTCA reports that a focus on cybersecurity assurance would evaluate the likelihood and consequences of cybersecurity failure. The likelihood of an attack takes into account different levels of trustworthiness of entities with access to a component and the relative intention to do harm. However, FAA officials and an aviation expert said that intention has not been considered a factor in avionics component-system failures because other security processes generally prevented untrusted entities from gaining access to avionics components. FAA officials said that the agency recognizes that cybersecurity is an increasingly important issue in the aircraft-operating environment and is shifting the certification focus to address this potential new threat.

FAA's Office of Safety began developing a larger airworthiness rule covering avionics cybersecurity in 2013 but determined more research was necessary before rulemaking could begin and halted the process. In December 2014, FAA tasked its Aviation Rulemaking Advisory Committee (ARAC) with submitting a report within 14 months of the March 2015 kickoff meeting that provides recommendations on rulemaking and policy, and guidance on best practices for information security protection for aircraft, including both certification of avionics software and hardware, and continued airworthiness. FAA states that without updates to regulations, policy, and guidance to address aircraft system information security/protection (ASISP), aircraft vulnerabilities may not be identified and mitigated in a timely manner, thus increasing exposure times to security threats. According to the ARAC task assignment, the report should provide recommendations by early 2016 on whether ASISP-related rulemaking, policy, and/or guidance on leading practices are needed, and the rationale behind such recommendations. If policy or guidance, or both, are needed, among other things, the report should specify which aircraft and airworthiness standards would be affected.

FAA Has Taken Steps to Clarify Cybersecurity Roles and Responsibilities, but Opportunity Exists for Further Action

Cybersecurity roles and responsibilities are spread across FAA among different offices with varying missions and functions related to cybersecurity. FAA is taking steps to align agency cybersecurity orders and policies, as well as IT infrastructure and governance, with the changing needs of the NextGen cyber environment. In November 2013, the Chief Information Officer (CIO) and Chief Information Security Officer (CISO) under the FAA's reorganized IT office began reorganizing and rewriting cybersecurity-related policies and plans agency-wide, and restructuring the agency's IT infrastructure and governance,[29] in part to address the shifts in cybersecurity activities and roles due to ATC modernization.[30] According to FAA, a working group expects to complete a draft by September 2015 that reflects the restructuring of IT infrastructure. The FAA's CIO is developing an enterprise approach for non-NAS information systems and cybersecurity, and is also leading a cross-agency team in developing the Cyber Security Strategy for 2016– 2020. Separately, the ATO is also developing and maintaining an enterprise approach for NAS systems in the ATC domain.[31]

FAA has also taken steps to better coordinate its cybersecurity efforts. FAA runs exercises that simulate cyber attacks and are designed to increase internal collaboration and help clarify roles during such events. Specifically, the NAS Security Risk Executive and other ATO staff organized and conducted five of these exercises between 2013 and 2015 involving FAA cybersecurity staff from different FAA offices as well as staff from the departments of Defense and Homeland Security, and MITRE. FAA officials said that these exercises are an integral part of sustaining and improving operational activities and are incorporated into the planning process for all NAS activities. FAA plans to continue conducting one or two per year.

In addition to the ATO's NAS Risk Executive, FAA established the Cybersecurity Steering Committee in November 2013 to better coordinate FAA agency-wide cybersecurity efforts at the executive level and provide an integrated approach to cybersecurity strategy and planning with a mission focus for FAA. The Committee has begun establishing the specific roles and responsibilities required to fulfill its mission. It is chaired by the CISO and includes representatives from ATO, NextGen, and Security and Hazardous Material Safety. These members are tasked with working together to identify, prioritize, strategize, and operationalize cybersecurity requirements, issues, programs, and projects needed to integrate an agency-wide approach to cybersecurity. Given that the Committee is in its early phases of operation, it is too early to tell whether it will be able to provide the cybersecurity visibility and coordination functions as outlined by the committee charter.

While FAA is working to transform the organization of its cybersecurity efforts, the experts we consulted said that it could improve upon those efforts by including all key stakeholders in its agency-wide approach. All 15 of our cybersecurity and aviation experts agreed that organizational clarity regarding roles, responsibilities, and accountability is key to ensuring cybersecurity across the organization. In addition, the five experts who commented on stakeholder inclusion all said that because aircraft avionics systems have the potential to be connected to systems outside the aircraft, aircraft cybersecurity issues should be included in an agency-wide cybersecurity effort. For instance, AVS issues cybersecurityrelated rules for aircraft and has begun reviewing rulemaking on cybersecurity, but AVS is not included in developing the agency-wide approach for information systems security and has no representative on the Cybersecurity Steering Committee. FAA states that AVS subject matter experts can be called upon to share information and recommendations but that regulatory aspects associated with cybersecurity for AVS's information systems are addressed by the FAA's CIO and are therefore not under the purview of the FAA Cybersecurity Steering Committee. While AVS has not directly requested to be on this committee, we previously found that it is important to ensure that relevant participants be included in collaborative efforts.[32] This lack of involvement could result in omitting an FAA stakeholder that has an understanding of specific technological changes in aircraft traversing the NAS environment and how these changes might intersect with changing ATC technologies and cybersecurity needs.

FAA's Acquisition Management Process Reflects Federal Guidance, but Management of Security Controls and Contractor Oversight Could Be Improved

According to NIST, one goal of an agency-wide approach to cybersecurity is protecting new information systems from threats by ensuring that when those systems are acquired, they incorporate security controls. To accomplish this goal, FAA's Acquisition Management System (AMS) includes the six major information-technology and security-riskmanagement activities described in key NIST guidance. [33] While FAA has integrated these six activities into the AMS lifecycle, our analysis of two NextGen foundational programs, SBSS and Data Comm, revealed instances in which some of these activities were not completed properly, or were completed in an untimely manner. In addition, while Data Comm managers have thus far provided oversight of their contractors' security-related acquisition activities, SBSS managers did not possess some of the detailed information that would have enhanced their oversight prior to the system's deployment.

FAA's Acquisition Management System Incorporates NIST's Information-Security Guidance throughout the Acquisition Life Cycle

To its credit, FAA has integrated NIST's six broad information-security and risk-management activities into its AMS, which guides the life cycle processes to be followed in developing FAA information systems. These activities include

- categorizing the system's impact level,[34]
- selecting security controls,
- implementing the security controls,
- assessing the security controls,
- authorizing the system to operate based on the results of security assessments and a determination of risk, and
- monitoring the efficacy of the security controls on an ongoing basis following a system's deployment.

These activities and their relationship to FAA's AMS life cycle are shown in figure 5 below.

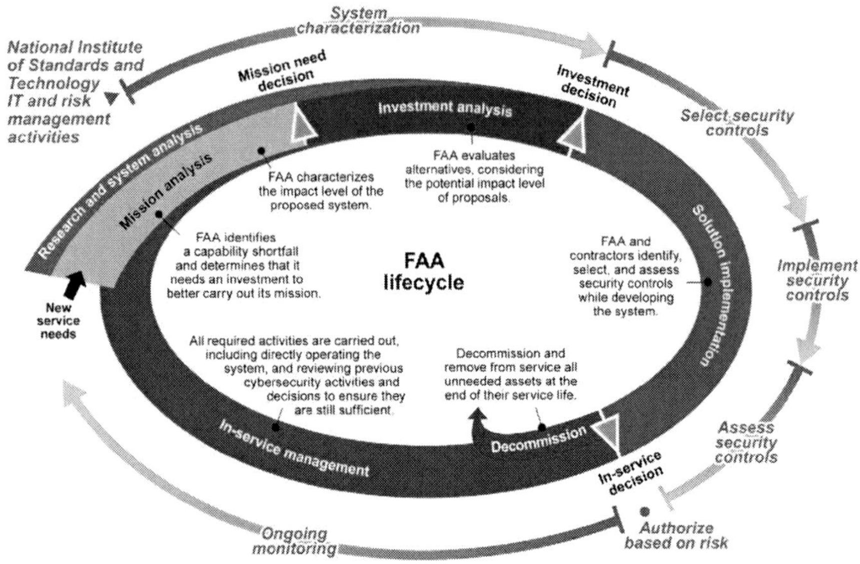

Source: GAO. | GAO-15-370.

Figure 5. Phases of the FAA's Acquisition Life Cycle and National Institute of Standards and Technology's Information-Technology and Risk-Management Activities.

System categorization: NIST guidance states that in applying the risk management framework to federal information systems' design and development processes, agencies should first categorize each information system's impact level (i.e., the severity of the consequences to the agency's mission if a system were compromised).[35] In accordance with this guidance and other federal agency requirements, FAA's acquisition process requires that each new system's security impact level be categorized as low, moderate, or high based upon the risks associated with the system and the information it processes, stores, or transmits.[36] Of the six foundational NextGen systems we reviewed, all have completed at least an initial categorization process.

Select security controls: NIST guidance states that agencies should next select protective measures, known as security controls, based on the characterization described above. 37 According to NIST guidance and federal agency requirements, the impact categorization determines which security control baseline (i.e., starting point for consideration) the system should use, as the low-impact baseline lists fewer controls than the moderate- or high-impact baselines. NIST guidance also states that as part of the selection phase, organizations should tailor the baseline security controls so that they align with the system's specific mission, function, or environment. In some cases, this aligning may include eliminating some inapplicable controls or applying supplemental controls. In accordance with NIST guidance, FAA's acquisition policies require the selection of appropriate security controls that reflect the system's categorization, and allow for appropriate tailoring of security controls. For example, detailed tailoring directions are provided in an FAA handbook that supplements the AMS. In addition, FAA recently drafted guidance to require that programs report, among other things, the cybersecurity decisions and activities conducted in the selection of security controls.

Implement security controls: NIST guidance also states that once selected, the system must implement controls specified in the security plan. The guidance emphasizes that implementation helps protect systems against possible compromise. When NIST changes its guidance and introduces new security controls, OMB calls for deployed systems to implement the controls within one year of the change, and for systems under development to comply with NIST publications upon their eventual deployment. The handbook that supplements FAA's AMS states that selected and tailored security controls should be implemented; however, according to FAA officials, FAA does not have a policy regarding how quickly to implement new NIST controls, and one official stated that the OMB's direction is "not realistic" given current constraints. The official noted that while the agency recognizes that its implementation cycle for critical cybersecurity controls needs to be more agile and responsive, swift implementation is hampered by federal-funding processes, acquisition requirements, and, as discussed below, the need to extensively test security controls. The official noted that FAA is considering adapting acquisition practices in order to rapidly implement critical controls; however, no definitive plan has been established.

Assess security controls: Additionally, NIST guidance states that assessments are important to ensuring that the security controls are functioning as intended. If a weakness is discovered during the assessment process, agencies are expected to generate a remediation plan to address the identified weakness. OMB directs agencies to develop plans of action and milestones (POA&Ms), which are intended to help agencies act upon assessment findings. Similarly, FAA's acquisition policies state that security controls should be assessed to ensure that they provide the necessary security protection for each acquired system. The FAA handbook that supplements the AMS provides detailed guidance on managing POA&Ms in the event that the assessments discover weaknesses.

Authorize system to operate based on risk: In addition, FAA's AMS states that systems must obtain security authorization approval prior to receiving authorization to operate, which reflects NIST guidance that authorization to deploy a system should only be granted after considering the risks. NIST guidance states the authorizing officials should consider the results of assessments, including POA&Ms, in their decisions. Similarly, the FAA acquisition process requires that the authorizing official receive POA&Ms to assist them in deciding if the system can be deployed. Moreover, the AMS requires that systems be reauthorized at least every 3 years, and the decision regarding whether or not the security risks are acceptable must be reconsidered at that time. According to both NIST and FAA policy, reauthorization may take place more frequently than every 3 years if significant changes occur to the information system environment.

Monitor security controls on ongoing basis: Last, NIST guidance states that agencies should monitor the security controls on an ongoing basis after deployment, including assessing controls' effectiveness and reporting on the security state of the system. FAA's AMS states that the security controls must be monitored after the system is deployed to ensure that they operate as expected and provide the necessary protection. Examples of FAA's continuous monitoring activities include periodic scans of operational systems, patching vulnerabilities, and updating the system's security plan. FAA's acquisition policies also require that each system assess a subset of its controls every year. Core security controls, which have greater volatility or importance to the organization, are to be assessed every year.[38]

We found that for all six NextGen foundational programs, FAA is addressing the broad security activities described in the AMS and NIST. The six programs are in various stages of the acquisition life cycle, which drives when security design and development activities should be done, as shown in figure 6 (below). For example, Common Support Services-Weather, and NAS Voice Switch are in the early stages of the life cycle, so some security activity milestones have not yet been reached. These two programs have only finished selecting their respective security controls. Other programs, such as SBSS, have performed all of the broad security activities at least once and are now in the post-deployment, ongoing monitoring phase.[39]

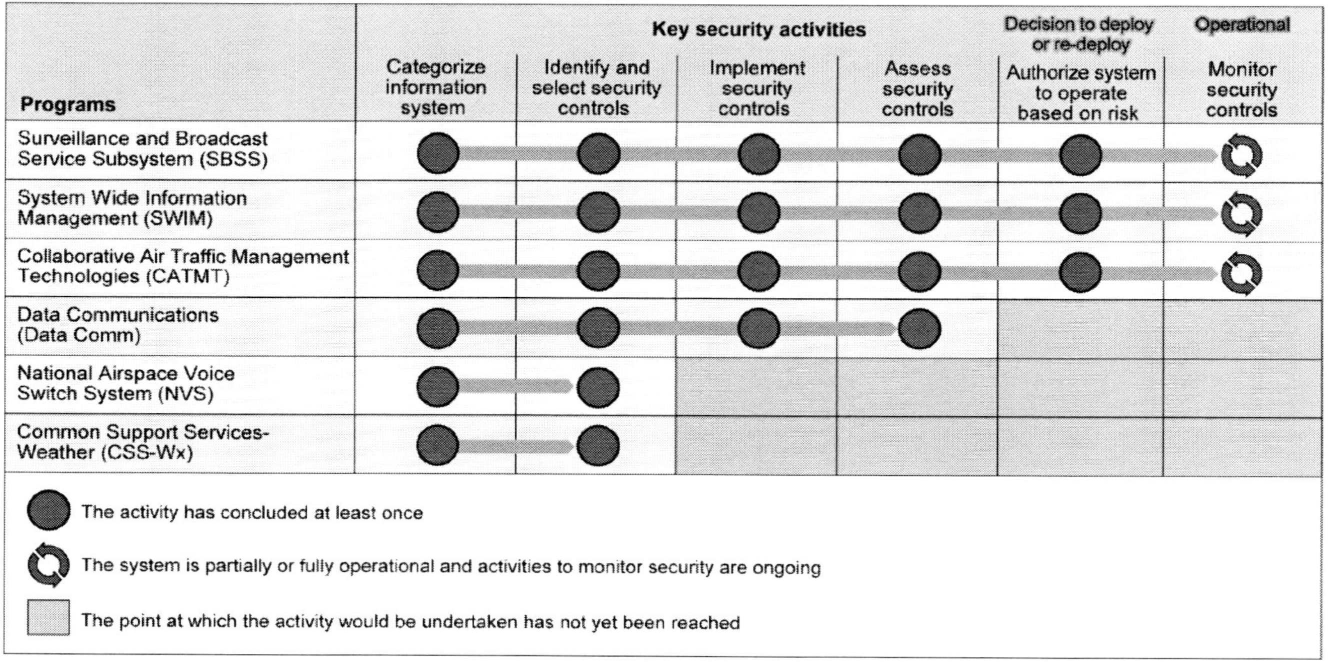

Source: GAO analysis based on FAA data. | GAO-15-370.

Figure 6. Security Activity's Progress for Each of NextGen's Foundational Program.

According to FAA policy, during the ongoing monitoring phase, some of the six broad activities will be reviewed or repeated to determine whether updates are required. For example, security controls for SBSS have been re-assessed by FAA's independent risk assessment team, which conducts testing, demonstrations, file reviews, and interviews with relevant personnel before and after a system becomes operational.

FAA Generally Followed Federal Guidance for Two Selected NextGen Programs, but Opportunities Exist for Improvement

Many of the six broad risk-management activities described in the AMS and NIST guidance involve security controls. These detailed protective measures—which include topics like access control, contingency planning, and physical security measures—are critical to ensuring that systems are sufficiently protected. Among other things, NIST guidance states that agencies should select security controls and assess the efficacy of security controls. In addition, NIST and OMB expect agencies to address weaknesses found during assessments. We analyzed two NextGen programs' treatment of security controls and remediation activities: (1) SBSS, which is operating in some parts of the NAS, including over the Gulf of Mexico, and (2) Data Comm, which has not yet finished the acquisition process but has deployed a test system. We selected these because of their importance to NextGen, cost, and deployment status. Although FAA adhered to aspects of federal guidance on control selection, assessment, and weakness remediation, its implementation of these risk management activities could be or could have been improved.

SBSS and Data Comm Generally Documented Security Control Selection Decisions, but Do Not Require the Most Recent NIST Controls

NIST provides the specific security protections, known as security controls that an organization should consider to help protect an information system.[40] For a "moderate impact" system, like the majority of the foundational NextGen systems that have completed the categorization process, NIST lists more than 200 such controls as a baseline. However, NIST acknowledges that agencies should tailor security controls so that they are relevant and appropriate for their individual systems. The process of tailoring controls can include electing to rely on common controls rather than selecting a comparable NIST control for implementation,[41] or deciding that controls identified by NIST are not applicable for a particular system. According to

NIST guidance, these decisions must be justified and appropriately documented, such as in a system security plan.

When SBSS was developed, FAA and its contractors selected controls from NIST guidance. For example, they selected controls such as an audit record of login attempts and automated mechanisms to alert security personnel to malicious activity. As allowed by the NIST and FAA guidance, SBSS determined that many controls were not applicable or were already covered by existing common controls, such as policies and procedures related to FAA security management activities. SBSS's initial system-security plan accounted for the majority of moderate baseline controls recommended at the time. However, it did not sufficiently document the implementation details for some controls, including contingency planning and incident response controls. For example, the initial system security plan described the existing process that FAA used to detect and respond to incidents affecting NAS systems. However, it did not describe system-level requirements or procedures for incident handling for SBSS. A few of these controls were associated with weaknesses identified during the assessment process, indicating that these controls should have received more consideration during the selection process. Better documentation in the system security plan may have supported such consideration. While FAA's system-security plan template from fiscal year 2009 provided guidance on documenting security controls, the fiscal year 2015 system-security plan template has since been updated based on NIST guidance and provides substantially more detailed instruction than in the past.

In addition, the 2008 SBSS system security plan did not record decisions associated with more than three dozen enhancements that NIST provides to strengthen the controls and that are included in the security baseline. For example, while the system security plan accounted for permitted actions without identification or authentication, it did not document the enhancement that clarified that actions should be permitted to the extent necessary to accomplish mission objectives. This lack of documentation may have been due to limitations in FAA's system security-plan template during that time period. While the template provided instruction that enhancements were to be documented, it did not specifically identify them in the same way that other controls were identified. SBSS continues to update the system security plan and security controls as part of the ongoing monitoring process, and the current system -security plan template covers enhancements.

The Data Comm program is newer than SBSS and is not yet operational, and as such, its initial security control selection is still under way.[42] As of October 2014, Data Comm had included approximately 60 percent of the more than 250 controls listed in the third version of the NIST 800-53 guidelines, some of which were identified as common controls. As for the slightly more than 100 controls that were identified as out of scope at this time, an FAA official explained that updates will be made as the program matures and that more security controls may be added in the future as deemed necessary. In accordance with NIST guidance, Data Comm has documented its justification for its current selection of NIST controls and its tailoring decisions to date in the system security plan.

However, even though SBSS and Data Comm contractors justify control selection in the programs' respective system-security plans, the contractors are not required to implement the most recent controls unless specifically tasked to do so by FAA. Currently, the SBSS contractor is only obligated to follow the first revision of NIST guidelines from 2006, although NIST has updated the guidelines three times since that time, most recently in 2013. Data Comm's contractor is required to follow the third version of the guidelines, which was published in 2009, and updated in 2010. NIST updates its guidelines to reflect new and emerging threats, and issues new security controls to help agencies better protect their systems. According to NIST, the most recent update was motivated by the increasing sophistication of cyber attacks and the operations tempo of adversaries (i.e., the frequency of such attacks, the technical competence of the attackers, and the persistence of targeting by attackers). According to FAA, systems can incorporate new controls on an ad-hoc basis or by modifying systems' contracts to reflect updated NIST guidance, and NIST's most recent controls are reflected in FAA's updated templates and guidance.[43] However, FAA does not require that contracts be modified within a particular time frame to reflect NIST revisions.

Although the SBSS program asks the contractor to implement more recent NIST controls on an ad-hoc basis, these actions are outside of the contract's requirements and, according to program officials, must be paid for separately. While ad-hoc additions may be sufficient in some cases, SBSS has not yet implemented some of the controls that NIST recommended in its 2010 revision, but plans to address these controls in accordance with NIST's 2013 update as these are part of a large update. SBSS officials explained that they did not previously have funding for an update of such a large scope, but they requested and received funding beginning in fiscal year 2015. According to program officials, these funds will allow them to adopt the missing controls. An FAA official stated that the SBSS program plans to adopt the most recent version of the NIST standards in fiscal year 2016. Given the pace of change in the threat environment, OMB is directing agencies that timely adoption of new

NIST guidance, within a year, is critical to enhancing the protection of agencies' information systems. As previously discussed, OMB requires that if NIST updates its security control guidance—which has occurred four times since the guidance was initially developed in 2005—deployed systems must implement all relevant updates within one year.[44] Systems with weaknesses that could be exploited by these adversaries may be at increased risk if relevant controls in the new NIST guidelines are not implemented.[45]

With regard to Data Comm, an FAA official responsible for the program explained that the program security office had reviewed the changes in the most recent version of the NIST guidelines and that the official did not believe any security control changes that warranted a contract modification.[46] Rather, the program will identify any security differences between the baseline and the latest NIST 800-53 revision 3 as part of the acquisition process and address them in the resulting POA&Ms, if required. However, the program office did not have an official analysis associated with this decision. NIST guidance recommends that agencies document the assumptions, constraints, and rationale supporting significant risk-management decisions in order to inform future decisions. Without documentation of its analysis, Data Comm's future managers may not be able to react appropriately when the threat landscape changes to such a degree that a contract modification would be warranted.

SBSS Did Not Sufficiently Assess Key Controls Prior to Deployment, a Lack Which Contributed to a System Outage

FAA did not sufficiently test certain security controls provided by the system's contractor prior to SBSS's deployment. As previously discussed, NIST guidance permits agencies to rely on controls provided by another party, such as a contractor; however, it instructs agencies to ensure that such controls are still sufficient and appropriate. As NIST explains and as GAO has previously found,[47] the responsibility for mitigating risks arising from the use of contractor-provided systems and security controls lies with the agency. NIST instructs agencies to determine if security controls provided by external parties are sufficient to ensure protection. While NIST guidance provides some latitude in how agencies are to accomplish this task, the guidance makes clear that the steps must be sufficient to ensure the security of the system at hand. However, FAA's pre-deployment testing of SBSS was insufficient. Specifically, according to the SBSS contractor, FAA used a briefing by the contractor to determine that the contractor's processes for managing and controlling changes to SBSS were sufficient. However, the agency did not evaluate the processes to ensure that they were in place and operating effectively until October 2009, nearly a year after the system was initially deployed, when FAA identified significant weaknesses with the SBSS configuration controls[48] implemented by the contractor.

Shortcomings in these contractor-provided change-management security controls contributed to a significant SBSS system outage. Specifically, in August 2010, an engineer made an error while implementing a system change that caused the network to shut down, which prevented surveillance data transmitted through the hub from reaching FAA control centers. As a result, air traffic controllers could not use SBSS surveillance data to help separate aircraft in the affected locations for nearly 16 hours. A report produced by the SBSS contractor after the outage identified that the outage had occurred because of shortcomings in the processes and controls for managing and controlling changes to the system, and recommended steps to ensure that such a disruption would not occur again, including strengthening these controls.[49] Although FAA's testing had discovered weaknesses in a few of the controls less than a year before the outage, more robust testing of the controls prior to deployment may have indentified these issues earlier—possibly allowing for any identified to be corrected in time to potentially prevent or reduce the impact of the outage. However, these weaknesses had not yet been remedied when the outage occurred.[50] FAA officials stated the outage has been thoroughly investigated to ensure that the SBSS program and the contractor learned from the experience, and that remedial actions were taken to strengthen the controls. Furthermore, a representative from the SBSS contractor noted that NextGen programs share information on an ad hoc basis to allow other systems to benefit from their experiences.

Although Data Comm has not finished selecting its security controls, an FAA official who manages the program reported that the contractor is testing controls that have been selected thus far. [51] In addition, Data Comm had identified more than 70 controls as of October 2014 that it classified as common controls. As previously discussed, common controls are managed by the agency, and accepting these controls is permitted by NIST guidance. According to FAA, Data Comm and other NextGen systems rely on the integrity of common controls so that they do not have to duplicate effort and spend funds needlessly. However, we recently reported that FAA did not test how some common controls protected the security of systems being added to the ATC environment.[52] For example, FAA defined the security awareness training common control, but the testers did not examine training records to verify that personnel on the systems that rely on the control were taking the training.

We recommended that FAA ensure that testing of security controls, including common controls, is comprehensive enough to determine whether these controls are operating effectively, and FAA concurred.

SBSS Did Not Consistently and in a Timely Manner Address System Weaknesses Discovered during Assessments

According to NIST guidance and the AMS, agencies are expected to create plans of action and milestones (POA&M) when security weaknesses are detected during the testing of an information system. According to NIST and OMB, POA&Ms are a remediation plan with milestone dates for corrective actions that are needed to mitigate the identified weakness.[53] In order for a POA&M to be closed, risk must be at an acceptable level. For example, the program might implement additional security controls, or further examination may show that the weakness is an acceptable risk or not actually applicable to the system. However, SBSS has not always remediated weaknesses identified in POA&Ms, which exposes the system to risk. According to FAA, SBSS was deployed in 2008 with weaknesses in the program's intrusion detection system, a shortcoming that was still unresolved as of early 2015. An FAA official explained that remedial actions had not been implemented previously due to a lack of funding, but would be applied as part of an estimated $42 million update in fiscal year 2015.

In addition, we recently reported 54 that current POA&Ms for four FAA programs, including SBSS, were not always addressed in a timely fashion. Of 26 SBSS POA&Ms that were completed during 2014, 25 were at least 6 months late, and 12 of these were more than 1 year late. For example, testing showed that certificates for many secure sockets layers, which facilitate secure connections between a server and a browser, had expired. Several FAA officials told us that timely resolution of POA&Ms had been an issue in previous years as well. According to ATO officials, one reason that original deadlines are often missed is that programs lack sufficient resources and funding to address weaknesses by their original due dates. In addition, prior to October 2013, programs used a POA&Mtracking system that one official described as "rudimentary." According to officials, the system only produced updates once a month, which was too infrequent to facilitate timely oversight and resolution of POA&Ms. In October 2013, FAA implemented a new POA&M database, known as the SMART Tool, that FAA officials say is intended to improve oversight, and could reduce delays in addressing POA&Ms.[55] Although FAA policy does not identify a maximum amount of time that a POA&M can remain unresolved, delays in addressing security weaknesses extend the amount of time that systems are vulnerable to exploitation. FAA officials agreed that systems are more secure when POA&Ms are resolved in a timely fashion.

In addition, until September 2014, Data Comm had not finished formally documenting the rationale as to why it did not plan to mitigate some of the weaknesses of a test system associated with the program. These weaknesses had been discovered in fiscal year 2013. Specifically, the Data Comm program is using a test system at two locations to obtain feedback from controllers, pilots, and other users. The test system generated 30 POA&Ms in fiscal year 2013, and FAA has since resolved them. However, FAA officials reported that they do not intend to address all of the POA&Ms because they will replace the test system in 2016 with new technology that reflects user feedback. All of the POA&Ms are categorized as "low risk," and FAA officials explained that their analysis of the costs, risks, and benefits indicates that these POA&Ms are not worth addressing given the replacement schedule; however, this analysis was not initially noted in the POA&M records. As noted previously, NIST guidance states that documenting significant risk management decisions is imperative in order for officials to have the necessary information to make credible, risk-based decisions. We asked Data Comm officials about this concern in September 2014, and were told that Data Comm had taken action to remedy the situation during the course of our audit. Specifically, the POA&M records were updated to reflect the program's decision process.

Oversight of the SBSS Contractors' Security Requirement Development and Security Control Implementation Was Lacking in Some Instances

According to FAA's AMS, procurement should be an integrated part of the acquisition life-cycle management process, and contract administration should include monitoring contract deliverables. We found that FAA and the SBSS contractor communicated about key milestones during the acquisition process, and such communication contributes to the broad goal of contract monitoring. For example, the contractor performed the design-phase risk assessment (which detailed the methodology for control selection), presented that assessment to FAA, and received comments from FAA on the control selection process. However, FAA's ability to monitor SBSS's contract deliverables was reduced by limitations in the system's work breakdown structure (WBS).[56]

A WBS deconstructs the program's end product into successive levels with smaller elements until the work has been subdivided into a level suitable for management control. The lowest, most detailed level of the WBS is defined as the work package level. There were more than 50 work packages for SBSS, but our analysis found that the work packages for SBSS primarily covered management issues for certification and accreditation versus detailed security issues. Consequently, most of the work packages did not address design and development activities for specific, complex, technical-security requirement areas. Moreover, many of the work packages' project implementation activities were not formally tracked or monitored. As a result of these issues, FAA could not effectively monitor the contractor's cost, schedule, and technical problems associated with specific security requirements. The lack of specificity and oversight unnecessarily increased the risk that weaknesses could occur.

SBSS's contractors are also responsible for implementing security controls to address weaknesses, but we found that in at least one case, FAA did not exercise its oversight responsibility to provide the contractor with sufficiently timely feedback on the plans of action (i.e., POA&Ms) that detail which security controls should be adopted. Specifically, in 2013, the contractor provided FAA with cost and schedule assessments associated with 48 POA&Ms. However, despite attempts to solicit feedback, FAA did not provide the contractor with timely feedback on this proposal for 5 months, when FAA declined the proposal. Instead, FAA determined it would issue a new request for proposals based on more recent NIST guidance (rev. 4) to address these controls.

As Data Comm is still under development, its security requirements and selected controls continue to evolve. Officials stated that they work closely with the contractor to ensure delivery against technical cost and schedule requirements. For the security controls selected thus far, FAA is able to trace the control to the associated security requirement, an ability that indicates that FAA is exercising oversight in this area. We also found that the Data Comm program also monitors system development and security through a variety of meetings, such as monthly Program Management reviews, quarterly Executive Committee meetings, biweekly Program Management Working Groups, and weekly Contracts meetings. While the AMS does not delineate specific meeting frequency or agenda requirements, the regularity and content from Data Comm's meetings aligns with the AMS guidance to monitor the contract deliverables.

CONCLUSION

Through its NextGen initiative, FAA is shifting the ATC system from a point-to-point communications system to an Internet-technology-based, interconnected system, a process of changeover that increases cybersecurity risks. FAA is making strides to address these risks, including implementing an enterprise approach for protecting its systems from cyber attack by both internal and external threats in accordance with NIST and other cybersecurity leading practices; however, FAA has not developed a holistic threat model that would describe the landscape of security risks to FAA's information systems. Such a model would inform the ongoing implementation of FAA's cybersecurity efforts to protect the National Airspace System. Development of a threat model could require significant resources and time, however, and FAA would first need to assess the costs and time frames involved in such an effort. FAA has also recognized that extensive changes to its information-security procedures and some realignment of information security functions within its organization are required to implement a secure, interconnected IP-based ATC system, and has taken a number of steps in this direction. However, the experts we consulted were concerned that FAA's plans for organizational realignment have not adequately considered the role of the Office of Safety, which is responsible for certifying the avionics systems aboard aircraft, including cybersecurity of those systems that enable communication with air traffic control and that guide aircraft.

FAA's acquisition management system is evolving to stay up-to-date on federal cybersecurity guidance as FAA designs and develops NextGen systems; and FAA has made significant strides in incorporating requirements for security controls recommended by NIST guidelines into its acquisition of these systems. While FAA generally followed many of the NIST guidelines for establishing security controls in the two key NextGen acquisitions we examined, we found instances where FAA lacked assurance that security weaknesses were properly addressed. For SBSS, FAA did not ensure that weaknesses identified during security reviews were adequately tracked and in some cases were not resolved on a timely basis. As a result, FAA lacked assurance that weaknesses that could compromise system security were addressed, exposing systems to potential compromise. FAA has taken steps to ensure future incidents do not occur, such as creating a more robust remediation system for tracking weaknesses. Also, for both systems, FAA has not yet adopted, as directed by OMB, the latest security controls recommended by NIST guidelines, which reflect updates to deal with the evolving cybersecurity threat to information. Although FAA anticipates that SBSS will adopt these controls in fiscal year 2016, the program has yet to provide the funding to the contractor to implement the controls. Delays in adopting the latest standards extend the amount of time that system security requirements may not adequately mitigate system exposure to the newest threats.

Recommendations

To better ensure that cybersecurity threats to NextGen systems are addressed, the Secretary of Transportation should instruct the FAA Administrator to take the following three actions.

- As a first step to developing an agency-wide threat model, assess the potential cost and timetable for developing such a threat model and the resources required to maintain it.
- Incorporate the Office of Safety into FAA's agency-wide approach by including it on the Cybersecurity Steering Committee.
- Given the challenges FAA faces in meeting OMB's guidance to implement the latest security controls in NIST's revised guidelines within one year of issuance, develop a plan to fund and implement the NIST revisions within OMB's time frames.

Agency Comments and Our Evaluation

We provided a draft of this report to the Department of Transportation for review and comment. The Department concurred with two of our three recommendations. Specifically, FAA concurred with the recommendation that it assess the potential cost and timetable for developing an agency-wide threat model, and the recommendation that it develop a plan to fund and implement NIST revisions within OMB timeframes.

With regard to the recommendation to incorporate the Office of Safety into FAA's agency-wide approach by including it as a member on the Cybersecurity Steering Committee, the Department believes that FAA has already complied with the intent of the recommendation. According to the Department, FAA has transferred cybersecurity personnel from the Office of Safety to the Office of the Chief Information Officer, which manages cybersecurity for all aviation safety information systems. The Department also stated that FAA's Chief Information Office works closely with the Office of Safety on certification standards for non-FAA information systems operating within the National Airspace System. We agree that these actions will help in the execution and coordination of cybersecurity activities involving the Office of Safety. However, we maintain that in addition to these actions, the Office of Safety should be a member of the Cybersecurity Steering Committee, which, as the department notes in its letter, was established to lead FAA's efforts to develop a comprehensive cyber-risk management strategy, and to identify and correct both existing and evolving vulnerabilities in all Internet protocol-based systems. Because aircraft aviation systems are becoming increasingly connected to systems outside the aircraft, the Office of Safety, which is responsible for certifying aircraft systems, should be involved in agency-wide cybersecurity efforts, including cybersecurity planning and vulnerability identification, since such efforts may be crucial in conducting its certification activities. As we state in the report, not including the Office of Safety as a full member of the Committee could hinder FAA's efforts to develop a coordinated, holistic, agency-wide approach to cybersecurity. This lack of involvement could result in omitting an FAA stakeholder that has an understanding of specific technological changes in aircraft traversing the NAS environment and how these changes might intersect with changing ATC technologies and cybersecurity needs.

In its comments the Department stated that FAA is committed to strengthening its capabilities to defend against new and evolving cybersecurity threats. According to the Department, FAA is initiating a comprehensive program to improve the cybersecurity defenses of the NAS infrastructure, as well as other mission critical systems. The Department's letter lists a number of actions FAA has taken to improve cybersecurity, many of which are described in this report. We applaud FAA's commitment to strengthening cybersecurity in the NAS, and agree that the actions it has taken are important steps for FAA to take. We also believe that addressing our recommendations will result in valuable improvements to the information security of the NAS.

Gerald L. Dillingham, Ph.D.
Director, Physical Infrastructure Issues

Gregory C. Wilshusen
Director, Information Security Issues

Nabajyoti Barkakati Ph.D.
Director, Center for Technology and Engineering

APPENDIX I: OBJECTIVES, SCOPE, AND METHODOLOGY

The objectives of this report were to (1) identify the key challenges facing FAA as it shifts to the NextGen ATC system and how FAA is addressing those challenges and (2) assess the extent FAA and its contractors followed federal guidelines for incorporating cybersecurity requirements in its acquisition of NextGen programs.

To ascertain challenges FAA faces with NextGen and how FAA has begun addressing these challenges, we obtained relevant security documents from FAA and detailed descriptions of FAA's cybersecurity efforts from officials. We also selected a non-generalizable sample of 15 cybersecurity and aviation experts with varied experience—some of whom have knowledge of FAA's internal cybersecurity activities, policies, and personnel. We then analyzed the information about FAA's cybersecurity efforts, synthesized it, and produced a document that we provided to the experts for their review. FAA concurred that the document was accurate. We then interviewed the experts, collecting information on the cybersecurity challenges they think FAA faces and will face in the NextGen transition. Interviewees also commented, to the extent they were able, on the extent to which FAA's cybersecurity activities and plans address the identified challenges. We analyzed and synthesized these responses, reporting on the numbers of experts who discussed particular topics as well as the numbers of experts who agreed or disagreed on particular messages. The experts from whom we obtained responses are listed in table 1.

Table 1. Experts Providing Responses to Cybersecurity Challenges Facing FAA

Expert	Organization	Title and position
John Knight, Ph.D.	University of Virginia	Professor, computer science
Steve Bellovin, Ph.D.	Columbia University	Professor, computer science

Table 1. (Continued)

Expert	Organization	Title and position
Rear Adm. Elizabeth Hight	Hewlett-Packard Company	Vice President, Cyber Security Solutions Group, U.S. Public Sector
Ed Skoudis	SANS Institute	Instructor/penetration tester
Phil Venables	Goldman Sachs	Chief Security Risk Officer
Dennis Sawyer	MITRE	Director, Aviation Systems Engineering and Center for Advanced Aviation Systems Development
Christopher Hegarty, Ph.D.	MITRE	Chief Scientist, Center for Advanced Aviation Systems Development
Barbara Endicott-Popovsky, Ph.D.	University of Washington	Director, Center for Information Assurance and Cybersecurity
David Shaw	Global Business Analysis	Founder, Chief Executive Officer
R. John Hansman, Ph.D.	MIT	Professor, Aeronautics and Astronautics and Engineering Systems
John Campbell	Iridium Communications	Chairman, Government Advisory Board
Richard Heinrich	Rockwell Collins	Director, Commercial Systems Strategy Development
Greg Rice	Rockwell Collins	Principal Cyber Security Engineer
Jeff Snyder	Raytheon	Vice President, Cyber Programs
Ronda Henning, Ph.D.	Harris Corporation	Senior Scientist for Security and Privacy

Source: GAO.| GAO-15-370.

Separately, we also obtained the views of several aviation industry officials, including officials from the Airlines for America, Airports Council International—North America, Air Line Pilots Association, General Aviation Manufacturers Association, Garmin, MITRE Corporation,[1] National Air Traffic Controller Association, and the Boeing Corporation. We also reviewed relevant reports issued by GAO, the Inspector General of the Department of Transportation, and the National Academies.

To assess the extent to which FAA and its contractors, in the acquisition of NextGen programs, have followed federal guidelines for incorporating cybersecurity controls, we compared pertinent FAA policies, procedures, and practices with selected federal information security laws and federal guidance, including standards and guidelines from the National Institute of Standards and Technology (NIST). In particular, we compared FAA's Acquisition Management System (AMS) against NIST's risk management guidelines and information technology-security guidelines (800-37) and security considerations in software development life cycle (800-64) to determine if FAA's acquisition policy follows federal cybersecurity guidelines for the six foundational NextGen programs: Surveillance and Broadcast Services (SBSS); Collaborative Air Traffic Management (CATM); Data Communications (Data Comm); NAS Voice Switch (NVS); Common Support Service-Weather (CSS-Wx); and System Wide Information Management (SWIM). The NextGen Foundational Programs consist of different segments, also called builds; parts; and subsystems. Some security activities take place at the program level, while others apply to specific components of the program. We analyzed FAA's program documentation of key cybersecurity activities as described by NIST and interviewed system managers to determine if FAA completed the activities or has plans to complete the activities that were started but not fully completed.

In addition, we chose two key NextGen acquisitions, SBSS and Data Comm, for an in-depth review because of their importance to NextGen, cost, and deployment status. SBSS has completed the acquisition cycle, while Data Comm will allow for insight into how the process has changed and what still might be an issue for upcoming programs. We assessed if FAA had established and implemented a disciplined life-cycle management approach integrated with information security by comparing FAA's policies for system life-cycle management and cybersecurity to NIST guidance on security risk management system acquisition. We also compared documentation of project activities and plans to these requirements, and interviewed officials about FAA's policies and FAA's information security practices. We assessed how well FAA and contractors completed key cybersecurity activities and the extent to which they complied with AMS and NIST requirements relating to cybersecurity. We also compared documentation of project activities and plans to these requirements, and interviewed agency officials about FAA's policies and information security practices. We also reviewed pertinent sections of prior GAO reports related to cybersecurity. We performed our work at FAA headquarters in Washington, D.C.; the Air Traffic Control Systems Command

Center in Warrenton, Virginia; and at an FAA contractor location in Herndon, Virginia.

We determined that information provided by the federal and nonfederal entities, such as the type of information contained within FAA's security assessments and Plans of Action and Milestones, was sufficiently reliable for the purposes of our review. To arrive at this assessment, we corroborated the information by comparing the plans with statements from relevant agency officials.

We conducted this performance audit from September 2013 through March 2015 in accordance with generally accepted government auditing standards. Those standards require that we plan and perform the audit to obtain sufficient, appropriate evidence to provide a reasonable basis for our findings and conclusions based on our audit objectives. We believe that the evidence obtained provides a reasonable basis for our findings and conclusions based on our audit objective.

End Notes

[1] US-CERT hosts the Department of Homeland Security's federal information-security incident center. When cybersecurity incidents occur, agencies are to notify the center.

[2] These 16 critical infrastructure sectors are: financial services; chemical; commercial facilities; communications; critical manufacturing; dams; defense industrial base; emergency services; energy; food and agriculture; government facilities; health care and public health; information technology; nuclear reactors, materials, and waste; transportation systems; and wastewater systems. White House, *Critical Infrastructure Security and Resilience*, Presidential Policy Directive/PPD-21 (Feb. 12, 2013).

[3] NIST is responsible for developing technical standards for the information-security programs across government.

[4] FAA's Acquisition Management System (AMS) provides policies and guidance for managing its acquisitions.

[5] NIST, *Guide for Applying the Risk Management Framework to Federal Information Systems: A Security Life Cycle Approach*, SP 800-37 Revision 1 (Gaithersburg, Md.: February 2010).

[6] NIST, *Security Considerations in the System Development Life Cycle*, SP 800-64 (Gaithersburg, Md.: October 2008).

[7] Internet Protocol, the principal communications protocol on which the Internet is based, is a networking technology that has been the industry's standard method to network computer systems since the late 1990s.

[8] According to FAA Order 1370.82A, the CIO appoints the Chief Information Security Officer—who is responsible for developing, implementing, and funding the agency Information Systems Security program—to provide security for agency information and information systems

[9] The ATO includes seven service units: Air Traffic Services, Management Services, Mission Support Services, Program Management Organization, Safety and Technical Training Services, Systems Operations Services, and Technical Operations Services.

[10] FAA created the ATO's NAS Security Risk Executive position in summer 2012, but the position description is still in draft form and is not yet codified in policy.

[11] Title III of the E-Government Act of 2002, Pub. L. No. 107-347, 116 Stat. 2946 as updated, by the Federal Information Security Modernization Act of 2014, Pub. L. No. 113- 283, 128 Stat. 3073 (codified at 44 U.S.C. §§ 3551 – 3558).

[12] Security controls are technical or administrative safeguards or countermeasures to avoid, counteract, or minimize loss or unavailability.

[13] FISMA was superseded by the Federal Information Technology Modernization Act of 2014, but FISMA retains requirements for agencies to implement an agency-wide information security program.

[14] NIST, *Guide for Applying the Risk Management Framework to Federal Information Systems: A Security Life Cycle Approach*, SP 800-37, Revision 1 (Gaithersburg, Md.: February 2010).

[15] NIST, *Security and Privacy Controls for Federal Information Systems and Organizations*, SP 800-53, Revision 4 (Gaithersburg, Md.: April 2013).

[16] National Institute of Standards and Technology, *Security Considerations in the System Development Life Cycle,* SP 800-64, Revision 2 (Gaithersburg, Md.: October 2008).

[17] OMB, *Management of Federal Automated Information Resources, Circular A-130* Revised.

[18] MITRE is a not-for-profit organization chartered to work in the public interest. MITRE manages four federally funded research and development centers, including one for FAA. MITRE has its own independent research and development program that explores new technologies and new uses of technologies to solve problems in the near term and in the future. MITRE has done extensive research on cybersecurity issues under contract for FAA.

[19] GAO, *Information Security: FAA Needs to Address Weaknesses in Air Traffic Control Systems*. GAO-15-221. (Washington DC: January 2015).

[20] Cybersecurity controls are safeguards or countermeasures to avoid, counteract, or minimize security risks relating to information systems.

[21] NIST recommends developing an organization-wide "risk frame" that establishes the context for risk-based decisions by identifying assumptions about the threats, vulnerabilities, consequences/impact, and likelihood of occurrence of cybersecurity incidents, which aligns with the threat modeling discussed by our experts. NIST, *Managing Information Security Risk: Organization, Mission, and Information System View*. SP 800- 39 (Gaithersburg, Md.: March 2011).

[22] The 2014 malicious insider attack on FAA's Aurora, Illinois, en-route facility, while not facilitated through cyber means, destroyed ATC IP and point-to-point telecommunications lines, preventing ATC electronic communications and the gathering and use of flight data, such as radar data, to track aircraft, resulting in over $350 million in financial losses to airlines.

[23] The Continuous Diagnostics and Mitigation program provides tools and services that enable federal and other government entities to strengthen the security posture of their cyber networks.

[24] GAO, *Information Security: FAA Needs to Address Weaknesses in Air Traffic Control Systems*. GAO-15-221. (Washington DC: January 2015).

[25] *Role-based* security permissions are based on a user's position or function within an organization.

[26] See GAO, *Aviation Safety: Certification and Approval Processes Are Generally Viewed as Working Well, but Better Evaluative Information Needed to Improve Efficiency*. GAO-11-14 (Washington, D.C.: Oct. 2010).

[27] *"Airworthy"* means the aircraft conforms to its type design and is in a condition for safe operation.

[28] Organized in 1935, the RTCA, which includes representatives from industry and FAA, is a private, not-for-profit corporation that develops consensus-based recommendations for communications, navigation, surveillance, and air-traffic management system issues.

[29] FAA created the Office of the Deputy Administrator for Information and Technology (AIT) in conjunction with the Office of the CIO. FAA IT Shared Services resides in this office.

[30] The FAA 2012 Reauthorization required FAA to undertake a thorough review of each program, office, and organization within FAA and to take actions as may be necessary to address the review's findings for, among other things, "reforming and streamlining inefficient processes so that the activities of the Administration are completed in an expedited and efficient manner." Pub. L. No. 112–95, §812, 126 Stat. 11, 124 (2012). One such action FAA has taken is to consolidate cybersecurity responsibility across FAA lines of business.

[31] Historically, before NAS information systems began the transition to IP networking, the Office of the Chief Information Officer, which sits outside of the Air Traffic Organization, had responsibility for NAS information system cybersecurity. Currently, the responsibilities of a security risk executive as described in NIST SP 800-39 are conducted for NAS systems by a position titled the NAS Security Risk Executive. The Cyber Security Steering Committee is in the process of developing policy that would center agency-wide risk executive responsibility in the Committee. Although the NAS Security Risk Executive position has been filled for about 2 years, the position description is still in draft form and the role has not been codified yet. The position does not control its own staff, nor does it receive specific funding.

[32] See GAO, *Managing for Results: Key Considerations for Implementing Interagency Collaborative Mechanisms.* GAO-12-1022. Washington, D.C.: September 2012). We recommended in 2006 that FAA be more collaborative and include all stakeholders in NextGen efforts as directed by Congress. See GAO, *Next Generation Air Transportation System: Progress and Challenges Associated with the Transformation of the National Airspace System*. GAO-07-25 (Washington, D.C.: November 2006). In response, FAA commented they planned to consider this recommendation.

[33] NIST SP800-37, *Guide to Applying the Risk Management Framework to Federal Information Systems: A Security Life Cycle Approach*, February 2010 and NIST SP 800- 64, *Security Considerations in the System Development Life Cycle*, October 2008. The former publication provides guidance for integrating security risk management activities into an organization's life cycle processes. The latter publication provides guidance on how essential information-technology security steps can be integrated into the life cycle. Steps that both publications have in common include system categorization; selecting, implementing and assessing security controls; authorizing the system to operate based on risk; and ongoing monitoring of the security controls. NIST guidance was developed to implement provisions of the Federal Information Security Management Act of 2002 (FISMA).

[34] *Security categorization* determinations consider potential adverse impacts to organizational operations, organizational assets, individuals, other organizations, and the Nation (SP 800-37).

[35] To determine the impact level of an information system, an agency must first determine the different types of information that the system processes, stores, or transmits. Then, for each information type, the agency categorizes the impact values for three security objectives: confidentiality, integrity, and availability. Last, the agency determines which of the three security objectives has the highest impact value—this "high water mark" measure is the overall information-system security categorization.

[36] This categorization process is required by Federal Information Processing Standards (FIPS) 199, *Standards for Security Categorization of Federal Information Systems.* FIPS 200, *Minimum Security Requirements for Federal Information and Information Systems*, states that agencies should use a minimum baseline of security controls based on the FIPS 199 categorization level. The minimum security baselines for each system categorization are defined in NIST 800-53, *Security and Privacy Controls for Federal Information Systems.*

[37] Examples of security controls include user identification processes, contingency planning, and the physical security of servers and other hardware.

[38] The Department of Transportation's Inspector General reported in November 2014 that FAA has not executed all elements of an effective continuous monitoring program. For example, the department has not implemented metrics or monitoring/assessment frequencies. However, the audit confirmed our finding that FAA has a policy for continuous monitoring. Department of Transportation: Office of Inspector General Audit Report FI2015-009. *FISMA 2014: DOT Has Made Progress But Significant Weaknesses in Its Information Security Remain*. (Washington DC: November 14, 2014.)

[39] NextGen programs are completed in stages, sometimes referred to as *builds*. As a result, even when one build of a system is operational, the program is not necessarily complete. New features and capabilities can be added to the system over time as future builds move through the acquisition process. Moreover, some steps can be completed more than once. For example, multiple assessments can take place.

[40] NIST, *Security and Privacy Controls for Federal Information Systems and Organizations*, SP 800-53, Revision 4 (Gaithersburg, Md.: April 2013).

[41] Common controls are "inheritable," and are therefore common for all the agency's systems (e.g., policies and procedures.) According to NIST, typically, these common controls are outside the direct control of the individual systems and programs, and are centrally maintained and managed.

[42] Data Comm is using a proof-of-concept device to operate a test system at two airports, Memphis and Newark. Although the test system completed certain security processes and received authorization to operate, officials explained that it is not Data Comm; rather, the test system is a tool being used to gather information that will inform the development of Data Comm. The Data Comm system itself is not operational.

[43] FAA updates its system-security authorization handbook yearly, and the October 2014 update reflects NIST's latest revision to the security controls in 2013.

[44] OMB also states that for information systems under development, agencies are expected to be in compliance with the NIST guidance immediately upon deployment of the information system. However, NIST guidance permits agencies to deploy systems even if weaknesses are known, so long as the risks associated with such weaknesses are acceptable to the agency. Agencies create plans of action and milestones (POA&Ms) to help monitor and address weaknesses found prior to deployment.

[45] NIST makes clear in its most recent guidance that its baseline protections should be considered a starting point for information security. Similarly, 8 of the 15 cybersecurity experts we consulted spoke about the protection offered by NIST guidance. All agreed that following

NIST guidelines was a necessary basic step, but noted that additional protections will be necessary to provide high-quality cybersecurity protection for NAS systems.

[46] According to NIST, there may be cases when a system's design and existing controls do not warrant a contract modification. For example, if NIST issues an update in response to new threats that do not apply to a particular system, or apply in a very limited manner and are addressed on an ad-hoc basis.

[47] GAO, *Information Security: Agencies Need to Improve Oversight of Contractor Controls*, GAO-14-612. (Washington DC: August 2014).

[48] Configuration management involves the identification and management of security features for all hardware, software, and firmware components of an information system at a given point and systematically controls changes to that configuration during the system's life cycle.

[49] FAA also produced a report in September 2010, which found that monitoring of the ground stations, communication between facilities, and training related to outage response could be improved. The Department of Transportation Inspector General reported in 2011 that FAA was taking action to improve these issues. Department of Transportation Office of Inspector General. AV-2011-149. *FAA Oversight Is Key for Contractor-Owned Air Traffic Control Systems That Are Not Certified* (Washington DC: Aug. 4, 2011).

[50] Untimely resolution of security weaknesses will be discussed in the next section of this report.

[51] Due to the iterative process of control selection and testing, we did not determine what percentage of controls had been tested.

[52] GAO, *Information Security: FAA Needs to Address Weaknesses in Air Traffic Control Systems*. GAO-15-221. (Washington DC: January 2015).

[53] POA&Ms can be generated at multiple points in the acquisition lifecycle. For example, they can be created during the system development and implementation phase; shortly before systems are presented for authorization to operate; or during ongoing monitoring and review.

[54] GAO, *Information Security: FAA Needs to Address Weaknesses in Air Traffic Control Systems*. GAO-15-221. (Washington DC: January 2015).

[55] According to FAA officials, information on open POA&Ms was completely migrated to the SMART Tool as of December 2013. Given the timing of our review, it was not possible to determine if the SMART Tool improved timeliness.

[56] A *work breakdown structure* is the cornerstone of every program because it defines the work to be performed and provides the means for measuring the deliverable's status. It provides a framework for estimating costs, developing schedules, identifying resources, and determining where risks may occur. Without a work breakdown structure, it would be much more difficult to analyze the root cause of cost, schedule, and technical problems.

End Note for Appendicx I

[1] MITRE is a not-for-profit organization chartered to work in the public interest. MITRE manages four federally funded research and development centers, including one for FAA. MITRE has its own independent research and development program that explores new technologies and new uses of technologies to solve problems in the near term and in the future.

INDEX

D

E

F

N

O

P

Q

R

S

T

U

V

W